Praise for *Brand The...*

"Brand Therapy is the 21st-century strategic marketing Bible for pharma and medtech brand leaders and their teams. It is an eye-opener for most of us still living in this industry's product-oriented, specialized culture as it offers new original models with lots of examples to think beyond the pill to prepare step-by-step powerful brand strategies to win." – Philippe Ghem, Senior Director, Marketing Excellence and Multichannel, Grünenthal GmbH

"The Health Check for your brand strategy. Simple and straightforward tools with lots of examples. Useful for beginners as well as experienced executives – an intelligent, accessible and comprehensive handbook." – Yves Ottiger, VP Global Marketing & Sales, B. Braun

"A masterclass in one book. Professor Brian Smith summarizes the key elements and particularities which drive the success of healthcare brands in just 209 pages." – Luciano Conde CEO, Noventure

"At last a book on marketing that perfectly fits the complexity and uniqueness of medtech and life sciences industries! More than just an academic marketing book, *Brand Therapy* provides simple and efficient tools to improve the relevance of marketing analysis and strategy building, tailored made for Medical Devices markets." – Sandrine Letellier, Vice President Global Marketing, Advanced Wound Devices, Smith & Nephew

"This is a book I would have loved to have in my pocket or my iPad earlier in my life in the pharmaceutical industry. It is amazing how Brian succeeds in sharing very important classical tools and enriches them to make them fit the market conditions we are facing nowadays… I hope all our colleagues in the industry will make *Brand Therapy* their daily handbook." – Anne Baille, Vice President Strategic Marketing

"A highly practical guide to the essentials of creating coherent and valuable brand strategy in medtech or pharma. It's a must read for anyone who leads or works in Brand Teams." – Craig Galloway, Associate Director International Marketing

"If you work in the pharma and medtech space and you have responsibilities for development and delivery of strong brand strategies, in today's complex and rapidly changing markets, there are very few appropriate and practical books to guide you. Until now. Prof. Brian Smith has condensed his 20 years of academic research into this step-by-step, brand strategy process which is tailored specifically for our unique customers and markets… I am certain I will be diving into this book many times over the coming years to utilise the many valuable techniques, tools and principles to strengthen the brands I manage. I read this book in a day and I believe every medtech manager should read this book and have it close to hand." – Kashif Ikram. MSc. M.A. MBA Senior Director EMEA Medtronic

"A must-read for every marketing manager in the pharma or med device space. This is the first book that I am aware of that looks closely at brand strategy specific to this industry. I have been reading Brian's work for a couple of years, and he gets it! He articulates in such a way that enables you to sort through the minutia and have that 'Aha' moment. It's easy for a marketing team to convince themselves that they have a better product than the competition, but to truly assess the strength of your strategy for a particular target market is the real litmus test. No one has given the easy to follow step by step methodology that he does before." – Linda Beneze, CEO at Monarch Medical Technologies

"Essential reading for every healthcare leader and brand team member who wants to create a successful, strong brand. Brian has translated the plethora of marketing literature into the healthcare context to make it relevant and current for the healthcare industry. Based on thorough research and repeated application he has come up with the tool-book for everyday use. Having prepared a brand for impactful entry into a very competitive market environment with the tools provided, I assure you: it works! The tool-book is essential to run the end-to-end strategy process in healthcare such as pharma or medtech. Also, it is a tool-box of choice to selected tools for testing, upscaling or fixing existing strategies." – Jens Thiedemann, Head of Marketing Europe, Daiichi Sankyo Europe

"This is a must read for any pharma/medtech professional about to kick-off a brand planning process. It is easy to read, but packed full of reminders regards well-established principles as well as new thinking. There is clarity in the 'red thread' that runs right through from understanding the environment to developing appropriate strategy and ultimately measuring the impact & taking the learnings of the tactics that are developed… with the specific relevance to pharma and medtech highlighted throughout." – Stephen Turley, Area Head, British & Irish Isles UCB Pharma

"This book stands out from many others in the strategic marketing area due to its focus specifically on the life science industry by an author who has extensive academic and industrial experience in life science. It will provide a wide range of brand, sales and marketing management readers with a set of tools that are based on academic research but uniquely brought together to aid the development of a robust, tested brand strategy fit for the complex market we compete in. This book is written in such a way that it can be used as a 'go-to' guide for brand strategy definition, development and verification." – Russell Watts, Director – Business Development and Marketing, EMEAI SCIEX, a Danaher company

"The need for 'innovative solutions' in a healthcare environment which requires disruption is high. Focusing on improved 'patient value' at a 'lower cost' – the industry must now be futuristic in how it responds. Smith has captured the new guide to brand relevance and sustainability." – Pamela Winsor Sr. Director Health Policy & Stakeholder Engagement Chief Marketing Officer Medtronic Canada

"This valuable handbook is a 'must have, must read and must use' for any anyone who wants to be successful in building Pharma or Medtech brand strategies. The scientific rigor used to build the theory combined with so many practical examples makes it easy to dip in and out of, and is spot on to sum up that in marketing everything begins and ends with the customer. Brand Therapy is a practical toolbox which will allow the Pharma and Medtech brand marketer to win the hearts and mind of their customers by defining the market from their point of view and addressing their needs better than anyone else." – Bharat Tewarie, MD, MBA, Executive Vice President and Chief Marketing Officer at UCB

Brand Therapy

*15 Techniques for Creating Brand
Strategy in Pharma and Medtech*

by
Brian D. Smith

academic rigour
pragmedic
pragmatic advice

First published in Great Britain by Practical Inspiration Publishing, 2018

© Brian D. Smith, 2018

The moral rights of the author have been asserted

ISBN (print): 978-1-78860-005-7
ISBN (ebook): 978-1-78860-006-4
ISBN (Kindle): 978-1-78860-004-0

Practical Inspiration
PUBLISHING

Contents

*Strong brand strategies come from using a set of complementary strategic
management tools in an integrated process. This chapter explains what tools are
available and their relevance to pharma and medtech markets.*

*You can't create a strong brand strategy until you really understand your market
and you can't understand your market until you define it the same way as your
customer does. This chapter guides you to begin your strategy making process with
a customer-centric definition of the market.*

*The brand team can only create a brand strategy if it first agrees on what one is.
This chapter defines what a brand strategy is and how it differs from the other
things with which it is often confused.*

Introduction

Is this book for you and why should you read it?
Why shouldn't you read another book?
Or none at all?

This book is for you if …

… you work in or with a brand team in a pharmaceutical, medical technology or other life sciences company. You might be a brand leader, senior or junior. You might work in sales management or medical affairs or market access or business intelligence or regulatory. You might work at Corporate HQ or in a national or regional affiliate. Different companies use different titles and structure themselves differently. Whatever your role, competing successfully in the life sciences market is difficult and requires a range of expertise, from medical and technological to marketing and other commercial. That's why almost all companies use cross-functional teams to manage their brands and products. If you work in one of those teams or aspire to, or if those teams report to you, then this book is written for you.

You should read this book because …

… successful brand management in medical technology, pharmaceutical and similar markets is very difficult. The products are technically advanced; the markets are very complex; and everything you do must be compliant with regulatory, legal and industry codes. In addition, the customers are very discerning and healthcare budgets are, and

1

always will be, very tight; demand for healthcare is more or less limitless, whilst the money to pay for it is extremely limited, whatever the product category. On top of this, you are competing with some of the best companies in the world. That's why you can't manage brands in this market by intuition and gut feel. You need tools and techniques to help your thinking.

Other books won't help you much in this market

There are thousands of books about strategic marketing planning. Amazon lists about 4,000. They all say much the same thing, although they try to differentiate themselves with new jargon and acronyms. Many of these books are good. But they are mostly written for and about very different markets—markets where the customer is an individual, not a complex of payer, patient and healthcare professional. They are mostly written for markets where you're free to say what you like about your product, without evidence, as long as it's not actually illegal. They aren't written for markets where marketing can be, quite literally, a matter of life and death.

You should read this book because your market is evolving rapidly

As I've written about in two of my previous books (*The Future of Pharma* and *Darwin's Medicine*), the life sciences industry, which includes pharmaceuticals, medical technology, diagnostics and other related sectors, is going through a spurt in its evolution. Huge changes are shaping the market. Compared to the recent past, the key strategic factors of who defines value, how they define value and how value is created by companies are all transforming rapidly. As a result, the industry landscape is fragmenting and its business models are evolving and differentiating. In this environment, your only chance to survive is to adapt. Your current approach to making brand strategy is as likely to hinder you as it is to help you.

So, this book is written for ...

... brand teams and their colleagues who need to compete in the complex, difficult, evolving life sciences market. It's based on my 20 years of rigorous academic research into that market, research that itself built on my preceding 20 years in R&D and marketing in pharmaceuticals and medical technology. In addition to that research and experience, it incorporates the lessons from hundreds of strategy workshops, brand planning projects and executive coaching assignments with many pharma and medtech companies, large and small. Both my research and my advisory work have encompassed companies and markets across the globe and this book is written to have similarly wide relevance. You don't have to read it. But, if your career and your company's success depends on you competing in pharma, medtech or related markets, you would be ill-advised not to.

Professor Brian D. Smith

Strong brand strategies use the right tools: An overview of the brand team's toolkit

Strong brand strategies come from using a set of complementary strategic management tools in an integrated process. This chapter explains what tools are available and their relevance to pharma and medtech markets.

A brand team in a pharmaceutical or medical technology company is an expensive thing. Think of how much it costs, not only directly in salaries, benefits and facilities but also what it spends on market research, marketing communications and myriad other expenses. This isn't money your company wants to spend. It's money your company feels it has a reason to spend.

That reason is a harsh commercial objective: to create and execute a brand strategy that delivers a good return on investment. So, a brand team's first, imperative goal is to create a strong brand strategy. Certainly, it also has a subsequent, important task to coordinate the implementation of that strategy across the company; but this book is mostly about the first task of creating a strong brand strategy. In the competitive, evolving

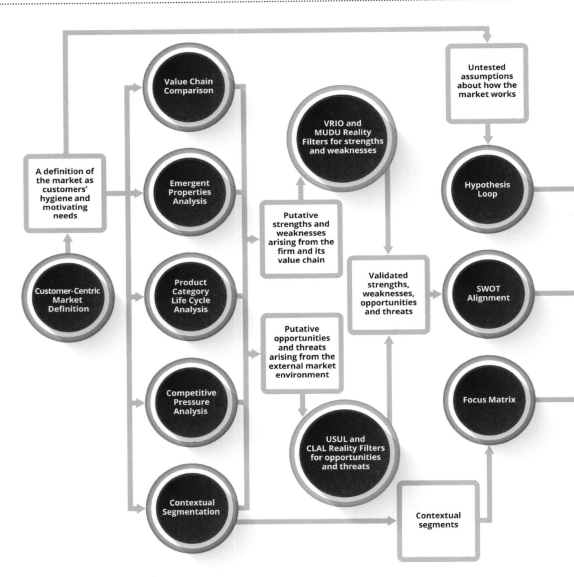

Figure 1.1 *An overview of the brand strategy process*

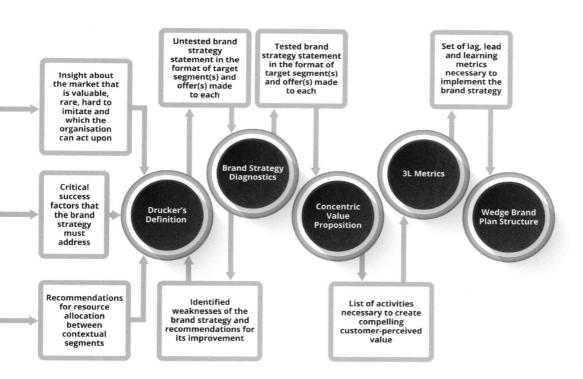

Insight about the market that is valuable, rare, hard to imitate and which the organisation can act upon

Critical success factors that the brand strategy must address

Recommendations for resource allocation between contextual segments

Untested brand strategy statement in the format of target segment(s) and offer(s) made to each

Tested brand strategy statement in the format of target segment(s) and offer(s) made to each

Set of lag, lead and learning metrics necessary to implement the brand strategy

Drucker's Definition

Brand Strategy Diagnostics

Concentric Value Proposition

3L Metrics

Wedge Brand Plan Structure

Identified weaknesses of the brand strategy and recommendations for its improvement

List of activities necessary to create compelling customer-perceived value markets in which pharma and medtech companies operate, this is a difficult task and you need a set of tools to do it well. The following chapters in this book are about the tools you can use to make strong brand strategy: what they do, how to use them and when to use them. But, as Figure 1.1 shows, this chapter is an overview of the whole process. It is about how those tools fit together to help you deliver what your company is paying the brand team to deliver: a strong brand strategy.

Chapter 2: Using the Customer-Centric Market Definition to frame your analysis

In simple markets, it can be enough to define your market in terms of the product you sell. It can be sufficient to say that you operate in the incontinence pad market, or the OTC analgesic market, where what's sold is a pretty good approximation of the market. But pharma and medtech markets are rarely simple. The market for many drugs, for example, is a fraction of the number of people who have the condition. The market for most imaging and diagnostic products is, in practice, only a part of the interlocking market for clinical information. Because markets and products are not the same thing, defining your market correctly is essential to first understanding it and then competing in it. The tool for doing this is the Customer-Centric Market Definition. How effective most of the other tools will be depends on defining the market correctly, so Chapter 2 describes how to use this tool before you do anything else.

Chapter 3: Using Drucker's Definition to clarify your brand strategy

In earlier times of relatively easy innovation and less constrained customers, pharma and medtech companies had relatively little need for strategy because their technological innovations almost sold themselves. As a result, strategy became a much-abused word. It was and still is often confused with tactics and objectives. Even when used separately from these things, it's not always clear what brand strategy is and how this is different from higher level and lower level strategies. This confusion over meaning is more than a matter of semantics. The lack of a shared terminology makes the brand strategy process less effective and less efficient. What's needed is a concise, clear definition of what the term brand strategy means. The tool for doing this is Drucker's Definition. It provides clarity about what brand strategy is and so, as Chapter 3 describes, should be used throughout the brand strategy process.

Chapter 4: Using Brand Strategy Diagnostics to test and improve your strategy

The history of pharma and medtech markets is one of technological breakthroughs—products like heart-lung machines, ACE inhibitors and immunoassays that were clearly and demonstrably better than the technologies that came before. With such radically innovative products, it was enough for a brand team to develop and deliver a list of imaginative tactics to inform the eager, expectant customer about the product and how it would address their unmet needs. But, in most parts of our modern market, those days are long gone. New products are usually incremental improvements over already good products. And even the rare, truly radical innovators find it hard to penetrate conservative, cash-strapped healthcare systems. This makes it essential to have a strong brand strategy, not merely a marketing communications plan. The tool for testing the strength of your brand strategy and ensuring it's as strong as possible is the Brand Strategy Diagnostic. Chapter 4 describes how it works and when to use it.

Chapter 5: Using SWOT Alignment to guide your brand strategy

The life sciences market has traditionally been less competitive than most. That may surprise you, but the evidence of gross margins, returns on investment and industry consolidation confirms it. Equally, recent waves of merger and acquisition, reducing margins and shareholder pressure tell us that this benign environment is changing rapidly, so demanding more competitive strategies. In essence, brand strategy is an alignment process so, when markets become more competitive, the challenge for brand teams is to align themselves ever more closely with the market. This means using their unique strengths to exploit market opportunities, and mitigating their equally unique weaknesses in the face of market threats. The tool for doing this is the much-misunderstood SWOT Alignment. Chapter 5 explains how to use this important tool correctly.

Chapter 6: Using Reality Filters to gain strategic objectivity

In less competitive times and in simpler markets, SWOT was used as a kind of bucket for collecting the brand team's thoughts. The inputs were often incomplete and usually subjective but, in those benign market conditions, that was good enough. Today's pharma and medtech markets are anything but benign. They demand effective SWOT Alignment, as described in Chapter 5; but this depends on validated inputs. The tool for testing and validating strengths, weaknesses, opportunities and threats before they go into the SWOT Alignment is a set of four Reality Filters. Chapter 6 explains what they are and how they work.

Chapter 7: Using the Focus Matrix to guide complex strategies

Pharma and medtech markets used to be driven primarily by the decisions of healthcare professionals such as doctors, nurses and technical staff. As a result, markets were relatively homogenous and a single approach to the entire market was sufficient to gain significant market share. That simpler old world is rapidly disappearing. Decision-making is now distributed amongst professionals, payers and patients who vary in both their tangible and intangible needs. This shift has caused many markets to split into segments that define value differently and offer very different returns on investment. This makes it necessary to allocate different amounts and different kinds of resources between those segments. The tool for doing this efficiently and effectively is the Focus Matrix, explained in Chapter 7.

Chapter 8: Using Value Chain Comparison to identify your firm's distinctive strengths and weaknesses

The early histories of many pharma and medtech companies are remarkably similar: pioneer founders (often scientists, doctors or engineers), following their dream to build a company that made a difference to patients and society. A logical consequence of this shared heritage was that the competitors in each sector of the market were often very similar in their technology, capabilities and organisational culture. But, in recent years, globalisation and growth have forced companies to specialise and differentiate so that even superficially similar companies operating in the same market usually have significantly different strengths and weaknesses. These differences are the basis for competitive advantage. The tool for identifying these important, idiosyncratic differences is the Value Chain Comparison, as described in Chapter 8.

Chapter 9: Using Competitive Pressure Analysis to identify competitive threats and opportunities

In pharma and medtech markets, it used to be sufficient to understand the competition as simply those firms making similar products and competing with you for share of the market. Competitive analysis was a relatively easy process of product comparison. But competitive intensity and technological complexity have combined to render this unsophisticated approach ineffective and insufficient for really understanding pharma and medtech markets. It's now necessary to understand the competitive pressures not only on your market share, but also on your profitability, and to identify threats from both direct and indirect competitors. The tool for doing this is Competitive Pressure Analysis, as described in Chapter 9.

Chapter 10: Using Contextual Segmentation to identify opportunities and threats from customer differences

When the customers of pharma and medtech companies were almost exclusively healthcare professionals, their shared training and mindset made markets relatively homogenous. Segmentation, such as it was, could be simplified into categories such as disease state or tier of healthcare. This is no longer true. The advent of payer influence and, increasingly, patient power, has rendered such straightforward categorisations much too simplistic. Competitive advantage now rests on understanding the variations in the contexts in which decisions are made. The tool for this is Contextual Segmentation, which is described and explained in Chapter 10.

Chapter 11: Using Emergent Properties Analysis to identify future opportunities and threats

The wider forces driving healthcare markets used to be understandable by the extrapolation of a few key factors: demographics drove the demand side, technology drove the supply side. In this simple environment, extrapolation of a small number of measurable trends was sufficient to predict the market. But many factors, from politics and economics to social trends and regulation, have now converged to render linear extrapolation obsolete and misleading. Instead, it's now necessary to understand how many different factors interact, leading to the emergence of both opportunities and threats. The tool for doing this is Emergent Properties Analysis, explained in Chapter 11.

Chapter 12: Using the Product Category Life Cycle to predict customer and competitor behaviour

Compared to today, pharma and medtech companies of the past were relatively flexible and adaptable. Product development cycles were measured in a handful of years and added value services could be developed in months. The costs and risks of innovative change were relatively low by today's standards. But market maturity, regulatory pressures and compliance issues have constrained companies to become much slower at adapting to market change, making pre-emption more important. It's essential to see into the future and anticipate how the market, especially the customer and competitor environment, will change. The tool for anticipating these changes is the Product Category Life Cycle, described in Chapter 12.

Chapter 13: Using the Hypothesis Loop to see what your competitors don't

The information that pharma and medtech companies needed to drive their brand strategies used to be relatively small in volume, simple in nature, and from a small number of sources. Demographics and disease patterns, competitor activity and customer purchasing behaviour were formerly quite sufficient to inform the brand plan. Today, the information revolution has changed that situation completely; the quantity and nature of the information available to brand teams is now much greater and it comes from qualitative and quantitative sources of baffling diversity. This creates the challenge of finding needles of insight in haystacks of data. The tool for doing this effectively is the Hypothesis Loop, described in Chapter 13.

Chapter 14: Using the Concentric Value Proposition to translate strategy into activities

In pharma and medtech companies, the process of translating strategy into activities used to be characterised by the phrase 'over the wall'. Strategy would be defined at a high level and 'thrown over the wall' to the brand team for implementation. There was minimal connection between strategising and execution. This was neither efficient nor effective but, in less competitive markets, it could be tolerated. Today, the demand for marketing effectiveness and accountability means that it's essential to translate brand strategy into actionable plans that are complete, internally coherent, consistent with strategy and fully costed. The tool for doing this is the Concentric Value Proposition, as described in Chapter 14.

Chapter 15: Using 3L Metrics to improve brand strategy implementation

In the context of a brand strategy, the term metrics used to be synonymous with expenditures and sales; information systems were set up to report these numbers, and brand plans were designed to give them visibility. But the weaknesses of this relatively straightforward approach have been exposed as pharma and medtech markets have become more competitive. Today, it's necessary not only to measure what was spent and what was sold; we need information that informs what corrective action must be taken during implementation, and that strengthens our assumptions for the next planning cycle. The tool to do this is 3L Metrics, which is described and explained in Chapter 15.

Chapter 16: Using the Wedge Brand Plan Structure to communicate your brand strategy

For decades, the structure of brand plans has remained essentially unchanged. Yet, over time, these brand plans have grown steadily as new details are added but unnecessary content is never deleted. The result is brand plans that often stretch for hundreds of pages, fail to communicate strategy effectively and are often left unread after the sign-off process. This is a wasted time cost in preparation and wasted opportunity cost in use, wastage that neither the brand team nor the company can afford. The tool for avoiding this waste and creating communicative, clear brand plans is the Wedge Brand Plan Structure, as described in Chapter 16.

These 15 tools comprise the essential toolkit for brand teams in pharma and medtech companies. Used collectively, as illustrated in Figure 1.1, these tools enable the brand team to work together to create strong brand strategies and gain their acceptance from their colleagues. In the following chapters, the application of each tool is explained succinctly in the context of the complex, competitive and changing life sciences market in which pharma and medtech companies operate.

Strong brand strategies are about the customer: Using the Customer-Centric Market Definition to frame your analysis

You can't create a strong brand strategy until you really understand your market and you can't understand your market until you define it the same way as your customer does. This chapter guides you to begin your strategy making process with a customer-centric definition of the market.

When should I use the Customer-Centric Market Definition?

You should always begin your brand strategy making process with a customer-centric definition of your market. There are a few, uncommon situations when doing so adds only a little value to the process but, in most cases, using this tool is time well spent. The inputs are very simple: your knowledge about who your customers are and what they're interested in. The output is a short, clear definition of the market in which you're competing. This helps focus the brand team and creates a solid foundation for all the other tools that you use. Brand strategies that are not built on Customer-Centric Market Definition are inherently weak, like a cathedral built on sand. For that reason, a Customer-Centric Market Definition is the first stage of your brand strategy process, as shown in Figure 2.1.

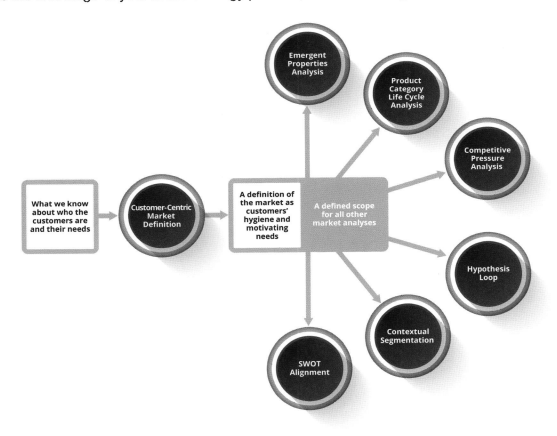

Figure 2.1 *Where the Customer-Centric Market Definition fits into the brand strategy process*

Why is the Customer-Centric Market Definition especially important in pharma and medtech markets?

Pharma and medtech markets have their origins in, and are still dominated by, a product-centric view of the world. For the most part, their founders were doctors, pharmacists, engineers, scientists or other similar professionals. For much of their history, and especially the last few decades, pharma and medtech companies have competed mostly by inventing innovative new products. This history has led most companies in the industry to have a strongly product-oriented culture. If you need evidence of that, look out for what management scientists call the visible artefacts of your company culture. For example, you will see that companies are often organised around product categories and management reports of spending and income are usually structured by brand. Everywhere you go in a pharma or medtech company, you can see obvious and less obvious examples of a product-oriented culture. It's often easier to see in other company cultures than in your own because, as is often said, employees are as aware of their company culture as a fish is of the water in which it swims.

Another artefact of this product-oriented culture is the way companies typically define their market in product terms. Market data, for example, usually defines the market size as the aggregate of all the products sold in that market. Competitors are usually defined as other firms who make the same product type. Customers are those who currently buy from us or a competitor.

This product-based definition of the market weakens our understanding of the market in many important ways. In most pharma and medtech markets, product usage and the market for the product are very different things. Just think of the number of untreated patients with mental illness, for example. In addition, the competition may not be a similar product but a substitute, as talking therapies are in mental health. Finally, product-oriented market definition tends to focus attention on healthcare professionals when, increasingly, payers and patients play an important part in the decision-making process. By contrast, the Customer-Centric Market Definition leads to much more effective use of the tools for understanding the market, such as Contextual Segmentation (Chapter 10) and Emergent Properties Analysis (Chapter 11).

So, the Customer-Centric Market Definition is a valuable tool in any market, but it's especially valuable in pharma and medtech, where we're faced with a product-oriented culture, complex, latent markets, and changing decision makers.

What is the Customer-Centric Market Definition and how does it work?

Although it's now fashionable again, Customer-Centric Market Definition is an old idea. It emerged from the academic literature in the 1950s but, even then, it was a reflection of the practice of exemplary marketers in earlier decades. If you want a glimpse into its origins, the seminal read is Theodore Levitt's 1960 article, Marketing Myopia, in the *Harvard Business Review*. Despite a lot of hype and repackaging, the basic idea of customer-centricity is to look at the market from the perspective of the customer and not that of the supplier. Like most valuable ideas, customer-centricity is simple to describe but not so easy to do. When brand teams live and breathe their product, they find it hard to look at the market from another angle. In both difficulty and likely outcome, asking brand teams to be customer-centric is rather like asking parents to be objective about their children. However, the best brand teams do achieve a Customer-Centric Market Definition. They do so by following three questioning steps, even though they often do so unconsciously.

Step 1: What is the customers' most fundamental need?

Customer-centricity begins with asking why anybody might ever be your customer. In other words, what fundamental need would anyone be seeking to meet if they were in the market? There's a judgement call to be made here, as shown in Figure 2.2. It's too narrow a view to say, 'They have a need for my product' because, in most pharma and medtech markets, customers would prefer not to buy the product at all. Nobody wants to buy an anticoagulant, a CT scanner or an immunoassay instrument. They all want to meet a need, such as stroke prevention or diagnostic information. On the other hand, it's possible to go too far the other way and say that the ultimate need of everyone is good health. Too narrow a definition of customer needs leads to the product-orientation problems mentioned above, too wide a definition leads to a market analysis that is too broad to be practically useful.

Exercise 2.1

Imagine being one of your customers or potential customers and being asked what you need. Try to answer without mentioning a product of any kind. A strong answer would be a need that is shared by all customers and that is different from customers in any other market. A weak answer would mention a product or be a need that only some customers have or that is generic to many different markets.

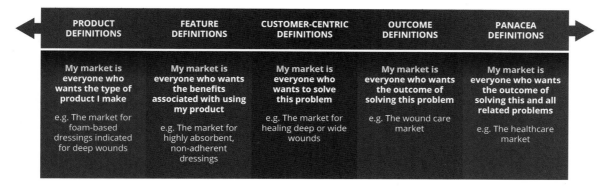

PRODUCT DEFINITIONS	FEATURE DEFINITIONS	CUSTOMER-CENTRIC DEFINITIONS	OUTCOME DEFINITIONS	PANACEA DEFINITIONS
My market is everyone who wants the type of product I make	My market is everyone who wants the benefits associated with using my product	My market is everyone who wants to solve this problem	My market is everyone who wants the outcome of solving this problem	My market is everyone who wants the outcome of solving this and all related problems
e.g. The market for foam-based dressings indicated for deep wounds	e.g. The market for highly absorbent, non-adherent dressings	e.g. The market for healing deep or wide wounds	e.g. The wound care market	e.g. The healthcare market

Figure 2.2 *The spectrum of market definitions*

The balance point is achieved by looking through the customers' eyes and imagining, for a moment, that products don't exist. What need has brought a customer to the market? The answer will be somewhere between seeking a product and seeking the panacea of good health. For example, it might be 'I want to control coagulation' or 'I want to prevent deep vein thrombosis' or 'I want to detect cancers early'. Importantly, this fundamental need must be what motivates them to buy products or services; but it's not a product or service.

Step 2: Who are the customers?

Exercise 2.2

Beginning with the fundamental need you identified earlier in Exercise 2.1, list all those people involved in addressing that need. A good answer would include specific descriptions of the payers, patients and professionals involved. A weak answer would either omit some people who are involved in addressing that need or include people who may have an interest but are not significantly involved in the choice of how to address that need.

Having clarified the fundamental need that brings customers into the market, the next step in developing a customer-centric definition of the market is to be clear on who these customers are. The unusual structure of pharma and medtech markets makes this question more complicated than it would be in the market for consumer goods, for example. This is because life sciences markets are almost unique in that the person who pays, the person who uses and the person who consumes are often different people, with very different needs and perspectives. Although the relative influence of each varies greatly between markets and product categories, most pharma and medtech markets involve payers, professionals and patients. Since they are all involved in addressing the fundamental need, they are all customers. For example, in the market for wound healing, your customers might include carers, nursing staff, specialist tissue viability nurses, pharmacy managers, local purchasing committees and, possibly, national health technology assessors.

Step 3: What do our customers have in common and how do they differ?

Good answers to the questions in Steps 1 and 2 tell us who is in our market and why they are in our market. The next step in developing a Customer-Centric Market Definition is to characterise the market in more detail by defining and characterising the other needs that shape and shade customer behaviour as they seek to meet the fundamental need.

In practice, these other customer needs fall into two categories.

Hygiene needs

These are needs that are shared in equal degree by all customers in the market and that don't vary between customers. An example of a hygiene need might be that any way of meeting the fundamental need must be safe and reliable or that it must be easily accessible. The important thing about hygiene needs is that they're an 'entry price' into the market (you cannot compete without meeting them), but that they offer no competitive

Exercise 2.3

Based on the fundamental need you defined in Exercise 2.1 and using the list of customers you identified in Exercise 2.2, write a list of all the needs your customers have when they seek to satisfy their fundamental need. Then divide that list into two, hygiene needs and motivating needs, using the descriptions of those categories provided. Good answers will include both tangible and intangible needs of all customers and will differentiate well between hygiene and motivating needs. Weak answers will omit important needs or customers.

advantage (you cannot compete on the basis of meeting them), since every competitor in the market also meets those hygiene needs.

Motivating needs

These are needs that customers have in varying degrees, or some customers don't have at all. Motivating needs might be tangible, such as the level of efficacy in meeting the fundamental need. For example, some but not all wound-healing customers are motivated by the need to reduce pain, which is a common feature of dressing change. Or they may be less tangible, such as the need to feel innovative and pioneering in meeting that need. For example, some surgeons are motivated by the wish to be perceived as being at the leading edge of practice whilst others are more conservative. The important thing about motivating needs is that they differ between customers. They therefore form the basis for differentiating your offer to the market and your competitive advantage.

Exercise 2.4

Based on the outcomes of Exercises 2.1, 2.2 and 2.3 and using the example below as a guide, write a Customer-Centric Market Definition for your market. Good answers will include both who the customers are and their hygiene and motivating needs. Weak answers will be either product oriented or too broad to be practically useful.

Step 4: What is my Customer-Centric Market Definition?

After answering the questions in the first three steps, you should now be able to write a Customer-Centric Market Definition that has a generic form as follows:

We are in the (fundamental need) market, which includes (list of customers). This market is defined by the hygiene needs of... and the motivating needs of...

So, for example, one working example of a market definition in medical technology is:

We are in the market for the prevention, management and healing of chronic wounds, a market which includes patients and their carers, nursing staff, specialist tissue viability nurses, pharmacy managers and local purchasing committees. This market is defined by the hygiene needs for safety, quality, basic efficacy, basic affordability and ease of use in a community setting. Its motivating needs include applicability across a wide range of chronic wound types, demonstrability of health economic efficacy and minimisation of change of practice by nursing staff.

You can perhaps see how this market definition is an improvement on 'the absorbent dressings market' or the 'decubitus ulcer market,' both of which are typical in this sector.

What should I do with my Customer-Centric Market Definition?

Having written your Customer-Centric Market Definition, it should be the reference point for the rest of your process for making brand strategy. You should get agreement to the definition from the brand team and find ways to keep it at the front of their minds. Some companies have it framed and mounted on the office wall; others print it on the front of their working documents and brand plan. As well as framing the rest of the planning process, a Customer-Centric Market Definition helps to maintain focus and motivation because, unlike some other markets, it is personally fulfilling to work in pharma and medtech markets, which usually involve the relief of human suffering and add to wellbeing.

Pragmatic advice for brand leaders

You will be amazed at the pervasiveness and persistence of your product-oriented company culture and its power to pull you away from customer-centricity. For example, you might be tempted to define your market as a need for what your product does: 'We're in the blood-sugar monitoring market.' But this is just a form of product-oriented definition by the back door. (Why does the customer want to know this? Because they are in the diabetes management market.) Or you'll be seduced into thinking the customers you speak to most of the time are the only customers: 'The prescriber is the decision maker'. But this is a form of what psychologists call 'framing'. If the prescriber is the only decision maker, why doesn't each prescriber use only one product? Perhaps the patient is involved in the decision. As brand leader, you must challenge your market definition very strongly and work hard to avoid your culture creating group-think in the brand team.

CHAPTER 3

Strong brand strategies are decisive: Using Drucker's Definition to clarify your brand strategy

The brand team can only create a brand strategy if it first agrees on what one is. This chapter defines what a brand strategy is and how it differs from the other things with which it is often confused.

When should I use Drucker's Definition to clarify my brand strategy?

In pharma and medtech, it's common to use the term 'brand strategy' with the implicit assumption that everyone means the same thing by it. This assumption is almost always false; ask ten people for a definition of the term and you will get several different answers. The brand team can't begin work on what the brand strategy should be until they all agree what they mean by the term, so you should use Drucker's Definition whenever you use the term brand strategy.

It's quite rare to start brand planning from scratch. Most brand planning exercises begin with an outline strategy that has been passed on from R&D, corporate or from the previous planning cycle. The brand strategy is then refined and improved until it's finally agreed. Drucker's Definition should be used at every iteration to guide and direct the brand strategy process. But its most important use is when the brand strategy statement is developed from the outputs of the market analysis. The inputs for Drucker's Definition are your current ideas about how your brand will compete in the market, which come from SWOT Alignment (Chapter 5) and the Focus Matrix (Chapter 7) and sometimes the Hypothesis Loop (Chapter 13). The output is a brand strategy statement expressed in a particular form. Without this codification, it's impossible for the brand team to do its job of crafting brand strategy. In particular, the brand strategy statement becomes the input to the Brand Strategy Diagnostics tool (Chapter 4). The place of Drucker's Definition is summarised in Figure 3.1.

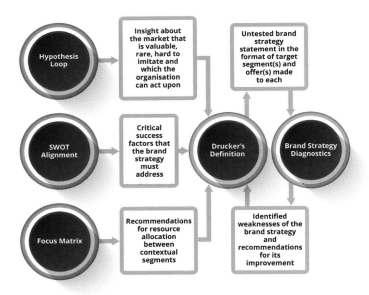

Figure 3.1 *Where Drucker's Definition fits into the brand strategy process*

Why is Drucker's Definition especially important in pharma and medtech markets?

Clarifying the brand strategy is important in all industries but it's particularly important in pharma and medtech because of the way that these brand teams work. In most other industries, the brand team leader is just that, a leader supported by a team. He or she 'calls the shots' about product design, pricing, channels, communications etc. By contrast, in pharma and medtech, the brand team leader is more of a facilitator. Responsibility for product claims is spread between medical, regulatory, marketing and R&D. Pricing levels and structure is often in the hands of market access but with finance looking on; channels are often the responsibility of sales; communication mostly lies with marketing but also compliance, and so on. Decision-making power is more dispersed than in most other industries.

This dispersion of power is necessary but it brings its own challenges. Different departments have different concerns and goals. They also have very different educational backgrounds and career histories. As a result, they have their own vocabularies and even when they use the same word they mean different things. A brand manager with an MBA may well use the word 'strategy' very differently from a medical affairs director. Sales teams and regulatory people will have their own interpretation of the term. Add to this the international, multilingual nature of many brand teams and it's not surprising that, when brand teams use the term 'brand strategy', they often share the words without sharing meaning.

In other words, the brand team of a pharma or medtech company can be something like a modern-day Tower of Babel and, just as in that biblical story, the brand strategy process can collapse because of failed communication. That's why Drucker's Definition is an essential tool in pharma and medtech.

What is Drucker's Definition and how does it work?

Drucker's Definition is an approach to defining the brand strategy using a specified format. It's necessary because many brand teams confuse brand strategy with either objectives, tactics, plans or other levels of strategy. For example, 'To be market leader in multiple sclerosis treatment with sales of $1bn' is an objective, not a strategy. It's what you want to achieve and says nothing about how you intend to achieve it. Similarly, when asked about brand strategy, many brand teams talk about tactics, some operational activity that is part of the strategy but not the whole strategy. For example, they may describe pricing (e.g. premium or competitive), product attributes (e.g. ease of use, efficacy, contraindications) or some aspect of marketing communications (e.g. 'our strategy is to raise awareness of the brand'). Most perplexing of all is when a brand strategy is confused with the entire brand plan, which is the often-voluminous document that records what the brand strategy is, why it was chosen and what activities will be done to execute it, amongst other things. Because of this confusion with objectives, tactics and plans, the brand strategy is often implicit, implied and unspoken. To be developed effectively, it must be made explicit and expressed in a clear form, which is the purpose of the Drucker's Definition tool.

An explicit brand strategy is simply a statement of resource allocation decisions about which market segment(s) to focus upon and what value proposition(s) to make to the segment (or to each segment). For instance, the brand strategy statement for a generic, broad-spectrum antibiotic might be 'to offer lowest cost, general use treatment of a broad spectrum of infections to the most price sensitive healthcare providers.' What defines this as a brand strategy is that it makes clear where resources will be allocated and where they will not. It makes clear that resources are to be allocated towards demonstrating low cost, general efficacy against a broad spectrum of bacterial infections to price sensitive customers, and not towards demonstrating specific use against a particular type of infection to customers concerned about efficacy or contraindications. Note that a brand strategy statement is always succinct and doesn't say anything about objectives or tactics, although the general direction of the latter may be strongly implied. In this example, lowest cost implies the general direction of pricing tactics.

Creating a brand strategy that is clear and succinct is a challenge that often eludes brand teams. Those that are good at it apply Drucker's Definition in three steps.

Step 1: What are and what are not our target segments?

The first step in applying Drucker's Definition is to state your target segment(s). This should include everyone you intend to target and anyone in the market you intend not to target. It should also clearly define those targets so they're recognisable. Staying with our simple but understandable example above, a simple statement of targets might be as follows:

> *We will target those healthcare providers with general but clinically undemanding requirements for the control of bacterial infection and whose behaviour is primarily driven by a desire for low cost.*

Exercise 3.1

Write a statement of your target and non-target market segments following the guidance given. A strong answer would be consistent with your Customer-Centric Market Definition from Exercise 2.4 and would define all your targets and non-targets clearly. A weak answer would be product oriented, would not define targets clearly and would fail to define non-targets.

We will not target those healthcare providers with specific and clinically demanding requirements for the control of bacterial infection and whose behaviour is primarily driven by those specific clinical needs.

31

Note that this statement uses a Customer-Centric Market Definition ('control of bacterial infection') developed in Chapter 2. It uses a non-product-oriented market definition and some of the motivating needs of that market.

Step 2: What are we offering to those targets?

Exercise 3.2

Write a statement of your offer(s) to your target market segment(s) developed in Exercise 3.1, following the guidance above. A strong answer will define clearly what you're offering and what you're not, in terms of benefits or value to the customer. A weak answer will fail to make clear what's being offered and not offered or will do so in terms of product rather than benefits or value.

The second step in applying Drucker's Definition is to state your offer(s) to the target segment(s). This must be a succinct statement that summarises the nature of the value being offered to the customer. It should also define what sort of value the offer doesn't involve. Again, using our simple example, a statement of the offer might be as follows:

We will offer the lowest-cost, effective control of a broad spectrum of bacterial infections.

We will not offer any degree of efficacy, freedom from contraindication or side effects that isn't available elsewhere.

Note that this offer statement is necessarily segment specific and would be quite different if it were for another target segment. Again, it's not product oriented and it's consistent with your Customer-Centric Market Definition (Chapter 2).

Step 3: What is our brand strategy?

The final step in applying Drucker's Definition is to combine the outcomes of the first two steps. This should result in a succinct statement that is your brand strategy. Continuing our simple example, a simple statement of the brand strategy might be as follows:

> *We will target those healthcare providers with general and clinically undemanding requirements for the control of bacterial infection and whose behaviour is primarily driven by a desire for low cost. To those customers, we will offer lowest-cost, effective control of a broad spectrum of bacterial infections. We will not target those healthcare providers with specific or clinically demanding requirements for the control of bacterial infection and whose behaviour is primarily driven by those specific clinical needs. We will not offer any degree of efficacy, freedom from contraindications or side effects that is not available elsewhere.*

Exercise 3.3

Combining the outputs of Exercises 3.1 and 3.2, write a statement of your brand strategy using the format of Drucker's Definition and following the guidance above. A strong answer will be consistent with your Customer-Centric Market Definition and make clear both your target and non-target segments, as well as what you will offer and won't offer. A weak answer will be product oriented and won't make clear your choices about how to compete in the market.

It's important to recognise that this example is for a very simple brand strategy that involves more or less binary choices between two segments. Most brand strategies are more complex and involve more nuanced allocation of resources between multiple segments. We will address this in Chapter 7, when we describe the Focus Matrix. But, even in complex brand strategies, the format of Drucker's Definition (target + offer) is necessary to allow the brand team to develop and improve the strategy.

Pragmatic advice for brand leaders

Developing Drucker's Definition of your brand strategy will meet two challenges. First, because brand strategy is confused with brand plan in many pharma and medtech companies, you'll encounter resistance to the idea that your brand strategy can be as simple as Drucker's Definition implies. As the brand strategy is discussed, there will be a tendency to play with the words and add to them until your brand strategy statement is long-winded and loses its meaning. It is the task of the brand leader to resist this drift to vagueness by emphasising that more detail will be added later in the plan but that the brand strategy statement must be succinct enough to be communicated clearly. Any brand strategy that cannot be read aloud in one breath should be challenged!

The second challenge will be a reluctance to say no. The brand team and others will find it much easier to agree who to target and what to offer than to agree who *not* to target and what *not* to offer. Many colleagues will want to chase every opportunity. Again, the brand leader must resist this tendency by pointing out that the whole point of strategy is to focus resources in order to maximise results. Focusing on everything is to focus on nothing; and if you focus on nothing you don't really have a brand strategy.

CHAPTER 4

Strong brand strategies are tested: Using Brand Strategy Diagnostics to test and improve your strategy

To do its job effectively, the brand team must be able to differentiate between strong and weak brand strategies. This chapter describes how to objectively test your brand strategy and identify where it can be improved.

When should I use Brand Strategy Diagnostics?

Brand Strategy Diagnostics is a useful tool to apply and reapply throughout the strategy making process. It is especially useful when applied at two points. First at the beginning of strategy making, when some outline strategy is implicit as the product begins to emerge from development. Then towards the end of the process, applied in an iterative loop to the output of Drucker's Definition, as summarised in Figure 4.1.

35

Figure 4.1 *Where Brand Strategy Diagnostics fits into the brand strategy process*

The input for Brand Strategy Diagnostics is your current brand strategy statement. The output is an objective and detailed assessment of how strong the brand strategy is, along with guidance about how it might be improved. Importantly, these outputs are shared amongst the brand team, helping form a common view of how the brand strategy needs to be improved.

Why is Brand Strategy Diagnostics especially important in pharma and medtech markets?

The history of pharma and medtech markets is one of inventing fabulous new products and selling them, mostly to relatively affluent governments. Compared to today, our products were easy to sell and our customers were well able to afford them. That is not to say that our predecessors had it easy, but the market of the first half of this century is quite different from that of the second half of the last. Technological and social forces have changed our market and will continue to do so.

This shift to a more competitive market environment increases the importance of brand strategy. In a market where your product is demonstrably superior and your customer is willing and able to pay for that superiority, you only need to be good at innovating and selling. This is especially true when your market is a relatively homogenous group of healthcare professionals, in broadly similar western healthcare systems, so that they all want much the same thing. This changes when the customers include payers and patients, who now seek value for money (not just efficacy), and when both competition and customers are global. In these new market conditions, innovation and selling remain necessary but are no longer sufficient. To thrive, you now need to be better at allocating your resources to optimise return on investment. And, at the level of the brand, resource allocation is just another name for brand strategy.

To put it bluntly, changing market conditions mean that 21st-century brand teams in pharma and medtech need to be better than their 20th-century predecessors. In particular, they need to be better at understanding what a good brand strategy looks like. That is why the Brand Strategy Diagnostics tool is especially important in pharma and medtech.

What is Brand Strategy Diagnostics and how does it work?

Brand Strategy Diagnostics is a method for identifying where and how you should strengthen your brand strategy. It was developed as part of a very large research project into the relationship between brand strategy and commercial outcomes. That research revealed that, although strategies vary enormously at a detailed level, strategy success or failure can almost always be attributed to one of five fundamental reasons. It's analogous to the findings of air-crash investigators when they examine flight recorders; although aircraft vary greatly in design and purpose, almost all crashes can be attributed to a small number of reasons. The corollary of this is that the probability of a successful flight can be greatly improved by checking just those key things. In the same way,

37

Exercise 4.1

Look at the target segment or segments in your brand strategy statement. Using the scale in Table 4.1, estimate the strength of your segment. Strong answers will objectively assess the homogeneity of the response expected from the target segment to a given offer. Weak answers will assume homogeneity of response without good reason.

Brand Strategy Diagnostics examines five key aspects of brand strategy before 'take off'; it guides corrective action, and makes it much more likely that the brand strategy will arrive successfully at its goals.

Brand Strategy Diagnostics begins by taking the brand strategy statement developed using Drucker's Definition. It doesn't work if the input is a statement of objectives or tactics rather than strategy. The tool then asks five simple questions, with the answers judged to range from 1 (very weak) to 5 (very strong). Finally, it uses those answers to guide how the strategy can be improved. This process is a skilled craft, not a simple checklist, and those firms that have mastered it do so in the following steps:

Step 1: Are our segments well defined?

Brand strategies succeed when the whole target segment responds positively to the offer. When only some of the segment does so, it means not only poorer results but also that some of your resources have been wasted. So, the first test of a strong brand strategy is to check that you've defined your target segment as a group who would all behave the same way to the same offer. This is assessed by comparing it to the five qualitative statements in Table 4.1.

Table 4.1 *Assessing your target segment definition*

TARGET SEGMENT TYPE	STRENGTH
A product, procedure or disease category (e.g. hip replacements, hypertension)	1 Very weak
A customer category (e.g. large hospital orthopaedic departments, large GP practices)	2 Weak
A user description (e.g. innovative orthopaedic surgeons, younger GPs)	3 Medium
A usage context (e.g. innovative orthopaedic surgeons performing difficult hip replacements, younger GPs with high-risk patients)	4 Strong
A decision context (e.g. innovative surgeons performing difficult hip replacements in an enlightened payer context, younger GPs with high-risk patients and high prescribing freedom)	5 Very strong

The important point is that an offer made in any given *decision context* is likely to get a similar response in almost all cases because the factors influencing the decision are the same in all cases. By contrast, the same offer made to a *disease category or customer category* will get a variety of responses because the factors influencing the decision vary within that category.

Step 2: Are our offers compelling?

Even if the target segment is well defined, brand strategies succeed only when the offer to each target segment is preferred to any competing offer. When it's not, or when there's no strong preference in any direction, the strategy will not achieve its objectives and the resources employed will have been wasted. So, the second test of a strong brand strategy is to determine how compelling the offer is, relative to any alternative the target segment might have. This is assessed by comparing it to the five qualitative statements in Table 4.2.

39

Table 4.2 *Assessing the strength of your offer to the target segment*

OFFER CHARACTERISTICS COMPARED TO ALTERNATIVE, AS PERCEIVED BY THE TARGET SEGMENT	STRENGTH
A greatly inferior offer (e.g. provides worse clinical outcomes at higher cost)	1 Very weak
An inferior offer (e.g. provides worse clinical outcomes at a similar cost)	2 Weak
A matching offer (e.g. provides similar clinical outcomes at similar cost)	3 Medium
A superior offer (e.g. provides better clinical outcomes at similar cost)	4 Strong
A greatly superior offer (e.g. provides better clinical outcomes at lower cost)	5 Very strong

Exercise 4.2

Look at the offer or offers in your brand strategy statement. Using the scale in Table 4.2, estimate the strength of your offer(s). Strong answers will objectively assess the attractiveness of the offer in the eyes of the target segment, relative to its alternatives. Weak answers will be subjectively biased towards your brand or will not consider the segment-specific motivations of the target.

The important point is that your target segment considers your offer in terms of how it meets their segment-specific needs and relative to any alternative, which may be a competitor or a substitute. The strength of your brand strategy is a function of both the strength of your target segment and the offer you make to it.

Step 3: Is our brand strategy different from our competitors'?

Brand strategies succeed when the segment you target and the value you offer to them is significantly different to that of the competition. This minimises direct competition and so creates localised superiority of resources. If this isn't done, market share tends to go in proportion to the resources spent and returns on investment are lowered. So, the third test of a strong brand strategy is its degree of differentiation compared to its competitors. This is assessed by comparing it to the five qualitative statements in Table 4.3.

Table 4.3 *Assessing the differentiation of your brand strategy*

BRAND STRATEGY DIFFERENTIATION COMPARED TO COMPETITORS	STRENGTH
A weak, undifferentiated strategy (e.g. very similar target segment and offer executed with less resource)	1 Very weak
A matching, undifferentiated strategy (e.g. very similar target segment and offer with similar resource)	2 Weak
A resource differentiated strategy (e.g. very similar target segment and offer with greater resource)	3 Medium
A strongly differentiated strategy (e.g. different target segment and offer with similar resource)	4 Strong
A completely differentiated strategy (e.g. different target segment and offer with greater resource)	5 Very strong

The important point is that brand strategies that compete for the same customers with similar offers get lower returns on investment compared to those that avoid head-on competition by targeting different customers with different offers. This ability to reduce direct competitive intensity is characteristic of all strong brand strategies.

Step 4: Does our brand strategy fit our organisation?

A brand strategy will be successful if you are more capable of executing it than anyone else. This means that your choice of target segment and offer should make good use of your organisation's particular strengths and either mitigate or correct its particular weaknesses. It's this alignment of internal strengths and weaknesses to external opportunities and threats that determines the relative ability of firms to execute strategy. So, the fourth test of brand strategy is the alignment between strengths and opportunities and weaknesses and threats. This is assessed by comparing it to the five qualitative statements in Table 4.4.

The important point is that unless the brand strategy fits your organisation better than it fits any competitor, the competitor will execute it better than you. This is why first movers are often beaten by market followers and why David sometimes beats Goliath. The strength of any brand strategy is a function of how well it fits the company trying to execute it.

Table 4.4 *Assessing the fit of your brand strategy with your organisation*

BRAND STRATEGY ALIGNMENT OF INTERNAL STRENGTHS AND WEAKNESSES TO EXTERNAL OPPORTUNITIES AND THREATS	STRENGTH
No alignment (e.g. the brand strategy fails to consider organisational strengths or weaknesses in its choice of target and offer)	1 Very weak
Weak alignment (e.g. the brand strategy considers organisational strengths and weaknesses but doesn't objectively assess them; they are therefore not allowed for in any significant degree)	2 Weak
Moderate alignment (e.g. the brand strategy coincidentally uses some organisational strengths or minimises some organisational weaknesses, but these are not objectively assessed)	3 Medium
Strong alignment (e.g. the brand strategy objectively assesses organisational strengths and weaknesses, but only some of these are used, corrected or mitigated by the choice of target and offer)	4 Strong
Very strong alignment (e.g. the brand strategy objectively assesses organisational strengths and weaknesses and all of these are used, corrected or mitigated by the choice of target and offer)	5 Very strong

Step 5: Does our brand strategy anticipate the future?

A brand strategy will be successful if it's written for tomorrow's market rather than yesterday's. This means that your choice of target segment and offer should allow for threats and opportunities that don't yet exist but are likely to emerge. It is this anticipation of how the market will change that determines the success of the strategy in changing markets. So, the fifth test of brand strategy is the degree to which emerging changes in the market are anticipated and allowed for. This can be assessed by comparing it to the five qualitative statements in Table 4.5.

Table 4.5 *Assessing how well your brand strategy anticipates the future*

BRAND STRATEGY ANTICIPATION OF EMERGENT MARKET OPPORTUNITIES AND THREATS	STRENGTH
No anticipation (e.g. the brand strategy doesn't consider any emergence of new opportunities or threats from the market)	1 Very weak
Minimal anticipation (e.g. some emergence of new opportunities and threats from the market is perceived, but these are neither objectively assessed nor allowed for in the brand strategy)	2 Weak
Moderate anticipation (e.g. some emergence of new opportunities and threats from the market is perceived, but these are not objectively assessed and only limited allowance is made in the brand strategy)	3 Medium
Strong anticipation (e.g. significant emergence of new opportunities and threats in the market is objectively assessed but only partly allowed for in the brand strategy)	4 Strong
Very strong anticipation (e.g. significant emergence of new opportunities and threats in the market is objectively assessed and fully allowed for in the brand strategy)	5 Very strong

The important point is that brand strategies must anticipate market change rather than react to it. This explains why previously successful brands decline and how disruptive new entrants can overturn powerful market leaders. The strength of any brand strategy is a function of how well it anticipates and allows for change in the market.

Step 6: What guidance does the Brand Strategy Diagnostic provide?

When you've completed the previous five steps, you will have an answer, ranging from very weak to very strong, for each question. This is the result of your Brand Strategy Diagnostic. You may choose to present it as qualitative text or numerically as a graph and you can consider the results both individually and combined into an aggregate 'health check' for your brand strategy. However you choose to present the results, it tells you what you need to do next. Where your brand strategy is less than very strong, you need to strengthen it by using other tools in this book. This guidance is summarised in Table 4.6.

Exercise 4.5

Look at your brand strategy statement. Using the scale in Table 4.5, estimate how much your brand strategy anticipates the emergence of new opportunities and threats. Strong answers will objectively assess both how well emergent changes have been assessed and the degree to which the brand strategy anticipates them. Weak answers will make subjective judgements of both factors and overstate the degree to which the strategy anticipates the future.

45

Table 4.6 *Guidance provided by the Brand Strategy Diagnostic*

AREA OF WEAKNESS OF THE BRAND STRATEGY	GUIDANCE
My segment definition is weak	Weak segment definition is at the root of most weak brand strategies. You should develop an understanding of the needs-based contextual segmentation in your market, as shown in Chapter 10.
My offer is weak	Assuming segment definition is strong, a weak offer usually reflects lack of insight into the market. You should develop some genuinely unique insight into the needs of your target segments, using the Hypothesis Loop tool in Chapter 13. A second, less common, reason for a weak offer is poor fit with the organisation (that is, you lack the strengths to make a good offer). If this is the case, see the guidance under 'My brand strategy doesn't fit my organisation'.
My brand strategy is undifferentiated	Lack of differentiation of brand strategy may stem from one of two root causes. If your target segment is undifferentiated, you should first use Contextual Segmentation (Chapter 10) and then use the Focus Matrix (Chapter 7) to review your targeting. If your offer is undifferentiated, you should use the Hypothesis Loop tool (Chapter 13) to review the insight it's based upon and then develop the Concentric Value Proposition (Chapter 14).
My brand strategy doesn't fit my organisation	Lack of fit arises from failure of the SWOT Alignment, which can be due to weak inputs or the alignment process itself. To improve the inputs, you should identify all possible strengths and weaknesses using the Value Chain Comparison (Chapter 8). You should look for opportunities and threats from Contextual Segmentation (Chapter 10), Competitive Pressure Analysis (Chapter 9) and from changes in the market place (using the tools in Chapters 11 and 12). The outputs of these tools should be filtered using the Reality Filters (Chapter 6) and the validated strengths, weaknesses, opportunities and threats aligned (Chapter 5).

AREA OF WEAKNESS OF THE BRAND STRATEGY	GUIDANCE
My brand strategy doesn't anticipate the future	Weak anticipation arises from failure to predict emergent changes in the market. You should anticipate changes by using Emergent Properties Analysis (Chapter 11), Competitive Pressures Analysis (Chapter 9) and the Product Category Life Cycle (Chapter 12).

What should I do with my Brand Strategy Diagnostic?

Each time you use the Brand Strategy Diagnostic, you will derive a list of actions involving the use of one or more of the tools in this book. You should use the diagnostic process, its results and the list of actions to build consensus on how to strengthen your brand strategy. In this way, this tool helps bind the team to a common purpose, without which they will tend to follow their own agendas. Once you've completed the actions, you should reformulate the brand strategy statement, again using Drucker's Definition (Chapter 3), and repeat the diagnostic. If done diligently, each iteration of the brand strategy will become stronger until there is little you can do to improve it.

Importantly, the strength of your brand strategy will now be demonstrable using the diagnostic questions. It will no longer be a matter of opinion. And once you have a

Exercise 4.6

Look at your answers from Exercises 4.1 to 4.5. Using the guidance in Table 4.6, prepare a prioritised list of activities involving the use of the tools in this book. Good answers will prioritise the areas of greatest weakness and use all the appropriate tools. Weak answers will focus on minor weaknesses and take action based on intuitive guesses rather than the use of tools.

strong brand strategy, you can develop the Concentric Value Proposition (Chapter 14), a set of 3L Metrics (Chapter 15) and a brand plan using the Wedge Brand Plan Structure (Chapter 16).

Pragmatic advice for brand leaders

Brand Strategy Diagnostics are a kind of truth serum. Used well, they strip away the subjectivity and vagueness that often accompany brand strategies. Revealing the reality in this way is very useful but, to loosely quote TS Eliot, humankind can't bear very much reality. You will therefore meet two kinds of resistance as your colleagues try to preserve their view of the truth. The first is that they will dispute the validity of the tests. You can refer them to the further reading but this won't change their minds because humans tend to distort information to fit how they want to see the world. This is what psychologists mean when they say we act 'to reduce cognitive dissonance.' A better approach is to discuss the premise on which the tests are built, which reveals that they are based on simple market realities. The second kind of resistance is subtler. When judging the answers to the questions in Steps 1 to 5, it's easy to be too kind to your strategy and assess it as better than it is in objective reality. Remind yourself and the team that this is counterproductive as the truth will eventually come out. It's your job as a brand leader to find and act on the truth about your brand strategy now. Leaving it to the market is a dereliction of your duty.

Strong brand strategies are aligned to the market: Using SWOT Alignment to guide your brand strategy

Strong brand strategies use your strengths to exploit opportunities and defend your weaknesses against threats. This chapter explains this alignment process and how it reveals the critical success factors that your brand strategy must address.

When should I use SWOT Alignment?

SWOT Alignment is the most misused of all strategic management tools. Part of this misuse is that it is used as a stand-alone technique when, in practice, it is a tool for processing the outputs of many other tools. You can't use SWOT Alignment correctly until you've completed at least the first iteration of Value Chain Comparison (Chapter 8), Competitive Pressure Analysis (Chapter 9), Contextual Segmentation (Chapter 10), Emergent Properties Analysis (Chapter 11) and the Product Category Life Cycle (Chapter 12). The outputs of those tools, once validated by the Reality Filters (Chapter 6), are aligned by the SWOT Alignment tool, whose output is a short list of critical success factors that your strategy must address. This list provides essential input into the Drucker's Definition of your brand strategy (Chapter 2) and also allows you to judge how well your strategy fits your organisation (see Chapter 4, Step 4). The position of SWOT Alignment in the brand strategy process is shown in Figure 5.1.

Figure 5.1 *Where SWOT Alignment fits into the brand strategy process*

Why is SWOT Alignment especially important in pharma and medtech markets?

The traditional focus of pharma and medtech companies is the development of more effective products for use by healthcare professionals. This emphasis evolved because, in earlier decades, it was successful. Product-focused companies were 'selected for' by the market, to use a Darwinian turn of phrase. But this approach has the disadvantage of narrowing our view, like a blinkered horse. We tend to see only those strengths and weaknesses associated with our products and only those opportunities and threats associated with rival products or, perhaps, our customers' view of those products. In our evolving market, where patients and payers are now as important as professionals, and value and service are now as important as technical or clinical efficacy, this narrow view often blindsides us. As a result, many pharma and medtech companies fail to understand the critical success factors that will determine the success or failure of their brand strategy. We see this when, for example, efficacious products fail to gain market access, when substitutes reduce the effective size of our market or when changes in the healthcare system leave our strategy behind. These are all symptoms of taking too narrow a view of the market; and pharma and medtech companies are particularly prone to these problems, with cultures that are a hangover from an earlier, simpler market. The solution is SWOT Alignment, which is a tool for drawing sense out of the complexity of the market. It's especially important in pharma and medtech markets because they're changing so quickly and because our product-oriented cultures lag behind those changes.

> *Exercise 5.1*
> **For your own brand and organisation, consider what validated strengths and weaknesses result from using the Reality Filters (Chapter 6). Write them down in the same form as shown in Table 5.1. Good answers will record five to ten strengths and weaknesses. Weak answers will use non-validated strengths and weaknesses or confuse these with external factors.**

What is SWOT Alignment and how does it work?

SWOT Alignment is often misnamed SWOT analysis. Correcting this small mistake is an important step towards understanding how to use the tool correctly. SWOT Alignment involves very little analysis. The analysis is mainly performed by the tools that provide SWOT Alignment with its inputs. Instead, SWOT Alignment is primarily a tool for processing the outputs of those earlier tools into valuable guidelines for your brand strategy. To be specific, SWOT Alignment is a process for finding the association between the company and its external environment. More specifically still, it is a process for aligning strengths to opportunities and weaknesses to threats, as shown in Figure 5.2.

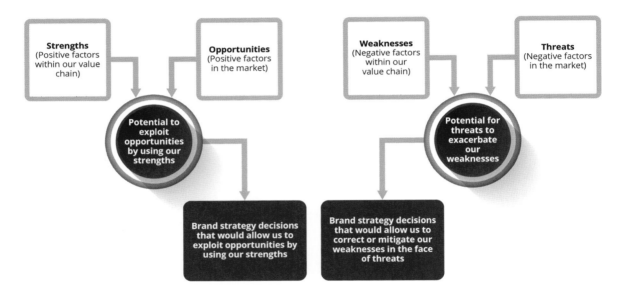

Figure 5.2 *The mechanism of SWOT Alignment*

As with all other strategic management tools, SWOT Alignment is not a mechanical, thoughtless process; there is a craft to performing it effectively. Those who have mastered this craft follow five steps.

Step 1: What are our strengths and weaknesses?

The first step of SWOT Alignment is to gather together the strengths and weaknesses already identified in the input analyses. Strengths are internal factors that have positive implications and have successfully passed the VRIO Reality Filter (Chapter 6). Weaknesses are internal factors that have negative implications and have successfully passed the MUDU Reality Filter (Chapter 6). The primary means of identifying strengths and weaknesses is the Value Chain Comparison (Chapter 8) although sometimes they're revealed by the Hypothesis Loop (Chapter 13). Strengths and weaknesses are usually tangible or intangible assets or capabilities that are, respectively, superior or inferior to those of the competition (see Table 5.1).

Table 5.1 *Examples of VRIO-validated strengths and MUDU-validated weaknesses*

VRIO-VALIDATED STRENGTHS
We can demonstrate that our unique, one-a-day posology improves patient compliance.
Our corporate brand and long-standing reputation in this disease area gives us access and share of attention to key opinion leaders at national and global level.
Our superior assets and expertise in social media and with patient advocacy groups gives us a greater capability to communicate directly with patients, within compliance constraints.

MUDU-VALIDATED WEAKNESSES
Our culture, structure and global pricing constraints make our unit price significantly higher than that of all major competitors.
Our unique use of X as a combination therapy is perceived negatively by some more traditional prescribers who have outdated concerns about the side effects of X.
Our breadth of portfolio and sales team structure mean that we have relatively small sales and marketing resources compared to our competitors and goals.

Step 2: What are the opportunities and threats?

Exercise 5.2

For your own brand and organisation, consider the validated opportunities and threats that result from using Competitive Pressure Analysis (Chapter 9), Contextual Segmentation (Chapter 10), Emergent Properties Analysis (Chapter 11) and the Product Category Life Cycle (Chapter 12), as well as the Hypothesis Loop (Chapter 13) and the Reality Filters (Chapter 6). Write them down in the same form as shown in Table 5.2. Good answers will record five to ten opportunities and threats. Weak answers will use non-validated opportunities and threats or confuse these with internal factors.

The second step of SWOT Alignment is to gather together the opportunities and threats already identified by preceding analyses. Opportunities are external factors that have positive implications and have successfully passed the CLAL Reality Filter (Chapter 6). Similarly, threats are external factors that have negative implications and have successfully passed the USUL Reality Filter (Chapter 6). Opportunities and threats are identified by those tools that analyse the various parts of the market environment, such as Competitive Pressure Analysis (Chapter 9), Contextual Segmentation (Chapter 10), Emergent Properties Analysis (Chapter 11) and the Product Category Life Cycle (Chapter 12). However, as with strengths and weaknesses, opportunities and threats are sometimes revealed by the Hypothesis Loop (Chapter 13). Opportunities and threats are typically the implications of market segmentation, competitive activity and emerging properties, as shown in Table 5.2.

Table 5.2 *Examples of CLAL-validated opportunities and USUL-validated threats*

CLAL-VALIDATED OPPORTUNITIES
There is a significant contextual segment in which compliance-related outcomes are the principal motivating need.
Our major competitor's reduction in size and refocusing of its sales team has left an influence vacuum amongst the 'cautious follower' contextual segment.
The spread of connectivity, information technology use and social media is creating a segment of actively interested and influential patients.

USUL-VALIDATED THREATS
Demographic, economic and political issues are creating a contextual segment in which preference is determined almost entirely on unit price, without consideration of wider value issues.
Competitor A's strategy is focused upon traditional prescribers with an offer that is reliant on the absence of X.
Approximately 45% of prescription decisions are made in contexts that are either price-driven or so strongly averse to X that we have little chance to influence brand choice.

Step 3: How do internal and external factors align?

The third step of SWOT Alignment is to align the strengths and weaknesses assembled in Step 1 with the opportunities and threats assembled in Step 2. Strategic alignment between internal and external factors occurs under one of two circumstances:

When a strength, or some combination of strengths, enables the exploitation of some market opportunity;

When a threat, or some combination of threats, causes the exacerbation of some weakness.

These situations are sometimes obvious but at other times are less so and, in practice, the process begins with finding the most self-evident alignments. For example:

> *'We have a significantly better side effect profile than any of our direct competitors.'*

would clearly align with

> *'There is a significant contextual segment that is primarily motivated by the desire to avoid side effects.'*

However, when obvious alignments such as these are completed, it's common to find strengths left unaligned to opportunities or threats unaligned to weaknesses. The second step is then to look for combinations that imply alignment. This process of alignment is iterative. In practice, it involves repeatedly attempting to find alignment and considering the ways that the different factors combine. The process is as valuable as the outcome, since it forces brand teams to think carefully about how they can compete. When complete, the alignment is laid out as in Table 5.3.

Table 5.3 *Alignment of strengths to opportunities and weaknesses to threats*

VRIO-VALIDATED STRENGTHS	CLAL-VALIDATED OPPORTUNITIES
We can demonstrate that our unique, one-a-day posology improves patient compliance.	There is a significant contextual segment in which compliance-related outcomes are the principal motivating need.
Our corporate brand and long-standing reputation in this disease area gives us access and share of attention to key opinion leaders at national and global level.	Our major competitor's reduction in size and refocusing of its sales team has left an influence vacuum amongst the 'cautious follower' contextual segment.
Our superior assets and expertise in social media and with patient advocacy groups give us a greater capability to communicate directly with patients, within compliance constraints.	The spread of connectivity, information technology use and social media is creating a segment of actively interested and influential patients.
MUDU-VALIDATED WEAKNESSES	**USUL-VALIDATED THREATS**
Our culture, structure and global pricing constraints make our unit price significantly higher than that of all major competitors.	Demographic, economic and political issues are creating a contextual segment in which preference is determined almost entirely on unit price, without consideration of wider value issues.
Our unique use of X as a combination therapy is perceived negatively by some more traditional prescribers who have outdated concerns about the side effects of X.	Competitor A's strategy is focused upon traditional prescribers with an offer that is reliant on the absence of X.
Our breadth of portfolio and sales team structure mean that we have relatively small sales and marketing resources compared to our competitors and goals.	Approximately 45% of prescription decisions are made in contexts that are either price-driven or so strongly averse to X that we have little chance to influence brand choice.

Step 4: What do we do about unaligned strengths, weaknesses, opportunities and threats?

It's not unusual, when the alignment process seems mostly complete, to find that there are still inputs into the SWOT that have not been aligned. You may find strengths with no opportunity to exploit and threats with no weakness to exacerbate. Or you may find the reverse: opportunities with no strength to exploit them, or weaknesses that are not exacerbated by any threat. If this happens, you have made one of two errors in the preceding steps and each error has a corrective action.

The more common error is when an input (a strength, weakness, opportunity or threat) has been entered into the SWOT Alignment without passing it through the Reality Filters. For example, if a perceived strength ('We have a 150-year history of manufacturing medical devices') has no corresponding opportunity with which it could be aligned (for example, there is no contextual segment that is driven by a need for manufacturing heritage), then this strength is not a strength. To correct for this issue, you should review how you applied the VRIO and MUDU tests. This usually reveals that the input should have been filtered out.

The less common error is the omission of an input, which occurs when the preceding input tools have not been used effectively. For example, if a strength such as 'robust design and manufacture' of a medical device passes the VRIO Reality Filter but there is

> ### Exercise 5.4
>
> **If the alignment you completed in Exercise 5.3 revealed any unaligned inputs, consider if this reveals either the erroneous inclusion or omission of an input. If the former, review how you used the Reality Filters. If the latter, review how you used the tools that provided the inputs, as described above. Reiterate your SWOT Alignment until you're confident it's complete. Good answers will align all strengths to opportunities and all threats to weaknesses. Weak answers will ignore this review and miss important alignments.**

no corresponding opportunity with which it could be aligned, then it may be that the Contextual Segmentation tool has not been used with sufficient rigour to identify a segment that would value this strength (such as a contextual segment where use is in mobile primary care in emerging markets). The same would be true if there appeared to be a 'missing' threat, which might imply some failing in the Competitive Pressure Analysis or Emerging Properties Analysis. You should review your use of other tools, but this time be sensitive to the 'missing' factor. For example, to whom did you think the non-aligned strength was valuable? Or why did you think the non-aligned threat was significant? This usually leads to finding the missing inputs and enabling you to complete the SWOT Alignment.

Once you've corrected these errors and either removed erroneous inputs or filled omissions, you'll probably need to reiterate Steps 3 and 4 until you're confident the alignment process is complete.

Step 5: What critical success factors does our alignment infer?

The final step of SWOT Alignment is to draw meaning from the alignments you've identified. Your goal here is to identify the 'so what' of the alignment between the internal and external factors. This is done by inserting a third, central column into the SWOT. This column must include a statement that makes clear how the strength should be used to exploit its aligned opportunity or how the weakness should be corrected or mitigated in order to avoid its exacerbation by its

> *Exercise 5.5*
>
> **Consider your completed alignment from Exercise 5.4 above. Insert and complete a third column, as in the example shown in Table 5.4. Strong answers will identify a clearly-expressed critical success factor for each alignment and these statements will, collectively, provide clear guidance to the brand strategy. Weak answers will fail to identify critical success factors or will fail to give clear strategic guidance.**

aligned threat. An illustration is shown in Table 5.4, developed using the examples in Tables 5.1, 5.2 and 5.3. When the third column is fully populated with clear, meaningful statements, the SWOT Alignment is complete.

Table 5.4 *Identifying the critical success factors implied by SWOT Alignment*

VRIO-VALIDATED STRENGTHS	A CRITICAL SUCCESS FACTOR FOR THIS BRAND STRATEGY IS THAT IT...	CLAL-VALIDATED OPPORTUNITIES
We can demonstrate that our unique, one-a-day posology improves patient compliance.	...will use our posology and compliance evidence to expand and win share of the compliance-motivated contextual segment.	There is a significant contextual segment in which compliance-related outcomes are the principal motivating need.
Our corporate brand and long-standing reputation in this disease area gives us access and share of attention to key opinion leaders at national and global level.	...will use our KOL-relationship assets to influence the neglected 'cautious follower' contextual segment.	Our major competitor's reduction in size and refocusing of its sales team has left an influence vacuum amongst the 'cautious follower' contextual segment.
Our superior assets and expertise in social media and with patient advocacy groups gives us a greater capability to communicate directly with patients, within compliance constraints.	...will use our patient communication capabilities to build trust and preference amongst actively interested patients.	The spread of connectivity, information technology use and social media is creating a segment of actively interested and influential patients.

MUDU-VALIDATED WEAKNESSES	A CRITICAL SUCCESS FACTOR FOR THIS BRAND STRATEGY IS THAT IT...	USUL-VALIDATED THREATS
Our culture, structure and global pricing constraints make our unit price significantly higher than that of all major competitors.	...will mitigate our pricing weaknesses by avoiding price-focused contextual segments.	Demographic, economic and political issues are creating a contextual segment in which preference is determined almost entirely on unit price, without consideration of wider value issues.
Our unique use of X as a combination therapy is perceived negatively by some more traditional prescribers who have outdated concerns about the side effects of X.	...will correct the perceptions of traditional prescribers by developing strong, evidence-based counterarguments.	Competitor A's strategy is focused upon traditional prescribers with an offer that is reliant on the absence of X.
Our breadth of portfolio and sales team structure mean that we have relatively small sales and marketing resources compared to our competitors and goals.	...will create localised superiority of sales and marketing resources by withdrawing effort from price-driven or X-averse contextual segments and focusing upon those seeking wider value, especially compliance-related value.	Approximately 45% of prescription decisions are made in contexts that are either price-driven or so strongly averse to X that we have little chance to influence brand choice.

What should I do with my SWOT Alignment?

The output of your SWOT Alignment is a short list of statements, usually between five and ten, beginning with 'A critical success factor for this brand strategy is that it...'

These critical success factor statements have two complementary uses. The first is that they can be used to direct the design of the brand strategy. In most cases, this list of statements gives a very strong indication of what your choice of target segments should be and what you should offer each of those targets. In this way, the outputs of the SWOT Alignment guide the choice of brand strategy made using Drucker's Definition (Chapter 3). The second use of the critical success factors is that they allow you to answer the fourth question in the Brand Strategy Diagnostics (Chapter 4), which pertains to fit (that is, alignment) between the organisation and the market. If your brand strategy fully addresses the critical success factors, you have a good fit. To the extent that those critical success factors are not addressed by the brand strategy, you have a poor fit.

Pragmatic advice for brand leaders

The biggest practical challenge in using the SWOT Alignment tool is that most of your colleagues will think they already understand it and that they have used it for years. They are most likely to be mistaken and will probably have been doing nothing more rigorous than randomly collating a set of untested and unaligned factors without identifying critical success factors.

In this case, the brand leader's first challenge will be to demonstrate that current practice is inadequate to the task in hand. The second challenge will be that rigorous SWOT Alignment reveals the weaknesses of the preceding analyses. When you begin to use SWOT Alignment rigorously, you'll find that very few things pass the Reality Filters, and so you'll have insufficient inputs to do SWOT Alignment well. This is most often true with strengths and weaknesses. Lack of validated inputs means that the preceding analyses have not been executed with sufficient rigour. In this case, your challenge as brand leader is to persuade your colleagues that their prior work was inadequate and must be reiterated. It is very likely that your colleagues will resist this idea. However, it is the job of the brand leader to remind the team that their task is to create strong brand strategy and that using the correct strategy tools, with rigour, is essential to that.

One other issue you might face is the suggestion to use strengths to offset threats. There are two reasons this doesn't work. Firstly, if a threat can be offset by a strength, that usually means it should fail the Unmitigated and Undefended tests from the USUL filter. Secondly, using a strength to defend against a threat is usually less cost effective than mitigating the weakness aligned to that threat. For example, you could use your low cost base (a strength) to reduce your prices and so defend against the threat that your competitor has better ease of use. But this would cost a significant part of your margin. The alternative actions would be to invest in improving the ease of use, (e.g. by design changes) or to mitigate the threat (e.g. by avoiding the small, 'ease of use is important' segment). A strategy that either mitigates or corrects a weakness is almost always better than one that erodes a strength.

CHAPTER 6

Strong brand strategies are based in reality: Using Reality Filters to gain strategic objectivity

The brand team's job is to make strategy for the real world, not the world as they would like it to be. This chapter shows you how to filter bias and subjectivity out of your market analysis so that your brand strategy is based on objective reality.

When should I use Reality Filters?

The Reality Filter tool should be used immediately before SWOT Alignment because using SWOT without the filters is the same as putting bad data into a powerful computer; you will get bad outputs that are more damaging because they seem more believable. The inputs into the Reality Filters are all the things we think may be strengths, weaknesses, opportunities and threats. These may come from the formal techniques described in this book, such as Value Chain Comparison (Chapter 8), Competitive Pressure Analysis (Chapter 9), Contextual Segmentation (Chapter 10), Emergent Properties Analysis (Chapter 11), the Product Category Life Cycle (Chapter 12) and sometimes the Hypothesis Loop (Chapter 13). Equally, you can supplement these inputs with your existing beliefs about strengths, weaknesses, opportunities and threats. If you use them well, the Reality Filters act as an acid test, discarding false perceptions and leaving only validated factors that can then be fed into the SWOT Alignment with much more confidence in the results. The place of Reality Filters in the brand strategy process is shown in Figure 6.1.

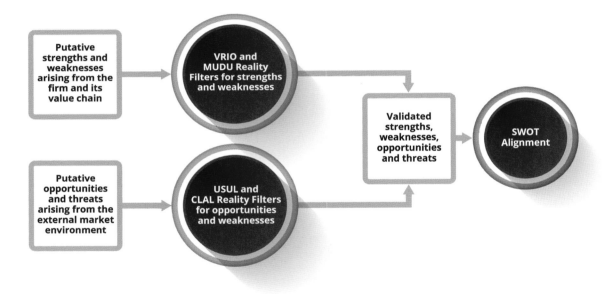

Figure 6.1 *Where the Reality Filters fit into the brand strategy process*

Why are Reality Filters especially important in pharma and medtech markets?

Reality filters are very important for any organisation that employs human beings, because we are flawed creatures with all kinds of cognitive weaknesses. Pharma and medtech companies especially benefit from using Reality Filters for market, technology and human reasons. Firstly, it is more than usually hard to make sense of the complexity of our market, with its conflicting needs, multiple stakeholders and convoluted decision processes. Add to that the increasing technological complexity of every part of the industry and you have a challenging sense-making task. This task falls to the brand team, people who are much more educated than average but who are still human, programmed by evolution to take mental shortcuts—heuristics—to make sense of the world. This mental software, designed to fit a hunter-gatherer world, works reasonably well, but leaves us prone to all sorts of cognitive faults, such as subjectivity, attribution bias, framing errors and so on. As markets become more complex, these cognitive faults become more of an issue, leaving us open to making mistakes. If you need evidence, look at all the products that are launched but fail or all the brand campaigns that waste money to little effect. The fact that we're trying to understand a 21st century market with Neolithic brains is what makes the Reality Filters especially important in the pharma and medtech industry.

What are the Reality Filters and how do they work?

The Reality Filters are a set of four separate but closely related tools, one each for testing strengths, weaknesses, opportunities and threats. Each sets four criteria that the putative strength, weakness, opportunity or threat must meet. If *all four* of these standards are met, then the factor passes the filter and can confidently be used as an input into SWOT Alignment (Chapter 5). If it fails, it may be rejected or it may be refined, restated and retested.

> ### Exercise 6.1
>
> **Gather together the putative strengths developed from your application of other strategy tools and other sources. Test each against the four criteria to determine which are VRIO validated. A strong answer will provide clear reasons for both the removal of some putative strengths and the retention of a small number of validated strengths. A weak answer will retain non-validated strengths.**

The Reality Filters are the offspring of two pieces of ground-breaking research. The first concerned the connection between brand strategy and commercial outcomes in pharma and medtech. This concluded that a vital difference between successful and unsuccessful brand strategies was in realism. Put simply, successful brands teams were more realistic whilst their unsuccessful rivals fell victim to their own cognitive biases. For example, brand teams routinely believe that their relatively expensive product, which offers no significant tangible advantages over their competitors, is in fact much better value than their much cheaper, very similar rivals. The second piece of research concerned the link between firms' resources and their commercial success. It found that success flows from leveraging resources that are valuable, rare, inimitable and aligned to the firm's other resources. Combining these two pieces of research together led to the Reality Filters, which are applied in four steps, although not necessarily in this sequence.

Step 1: Which of our perceived strengths are really strengths?

Starting with a collated list of perceived strengths from Value Chain Comparison (Chapter 8) or elsewhere, each perceived strength is tested by asking the four questions in Figure 6.2.

IS IT VALUABLE?

Genuine strengths are attributes that make the brand more valuable. For example, they may create customer preference (e.g. by superior technical performance or significantly lower cost in use) or enable higher margins (e.g. by lower operating costs). Attributes that do not make the brand more valuable (e.g. some feature of the product for which there is no demand or some aspect of service that does not influence customer preference) are not strengths, even if they meet the other three criteria for a strength.

IS IT RARE?

Genuine strengths are attributes that no other significant competitor has. For example, a brand may have a reputation for consistently high quality or a complete product range that enables purchasing concentration. Attributes that are commonly held by other competitors in the market, such as technical support or continuing medical education programmes, are not strengths, even if they meet the other three criteria for a strength.

VRIO Reality Filter for strengths

IS IT INIMITABLE?

Genuine strengths are attributes that cannot easily be imitated by a competitor. For example, the brand may be based on some strongly protected piece of intellectual property, a proprietary manufacturing process or a well-recognised brand. Attributes that could be imitated in the short to medium term, such as a lower price or larger sales team, are not strengths even if they meet the other three criteria for a strength.

IS IT ALIGNED TO THE ORGANISATION?

Genuine strengths are attributes that can be used without conflicting with the organisation's strategy, processes or other characteristics. For example, a capability to develop and maintain strong KOL relationships would be a strength for a research-based company but not for a generic manufacturer. By contrast, the capability to influence and win tenders and contracts in commoditised markets would be the reverse. Attributes whose use would conflict with the firm's strategy are not strengths even if they meet the other three criteria for a strength.

Figure 6.2 *The VRIO Reality Filter for strengths*

In most cases, these questions can be answered definitively and, in cases where this is not so, the discussion amongst the brand team is invaluable in building consensus. Most importantly, a strength is not a strength unless it meets *all four* criteria. For example, the ability to create and use real world data to support health economic claims may be very valuable, hard to imitate and entirely consistent with the rest of the organisation's activities; but if your major competitors have the same ability to broadly the same degree, it's not a strength because it doesn't meet the rarity criterion. Your strengths that meet all four criteria, are your VRIO-validated strengths. It is those that your brand must use to exploit market opportunities, as described in the SWOT Alignment process in Chapter 5.

Step 2: Which of our perceived weaknesses are really weaknesses?

As with strengths, filtering weaknesses begins with a collated list of perceived weaknesses from Value Chain Comparison (Chapter 8) or elsewhere. Each perceived weakness is tested by asking the four questions in Figure 6.3.

Again, these questions can usually be answered relatively easily, and the discussion amongst the brand team is valuable in building agreement. As before, a weakness is not a weakness unless it meets *all four* criteria. For example, the lack of health economic evidence to support the use of a premium-priced, Class IV, medical device may be important to customers, difficult to correct and not balanced by any other consideration

IS IT MEANINGFUL?

Genuine weaknesses are attributes that make a significant difference to the brand and the customer. For example, they may reduce customers' preference (e.g. by being significantly more difficult to comply with correct usage) or reduce margins (e.g. by having structurally higher marketing costs). Attributes that do not make a meaningful difference to the brand or the customer (e.g. some minor feature of the product design or minor contraindication that does not influence customer preference) are not weaknesses, even if they meet the other three criteria for a weakness.

IS IT UNCOMMON?

Genuine weaknesses are attributes from which no other significant competitor suffers. For example, a brand may have a reputation for side effects in some patient population or proprietary restriction on the use of consumables for instruments. Attributes that are shared with other competitors in the market, such as raw material costs or lack of availability of key staff, are not weaknesses, even if they meet the other three criteria for a weakness.

**MUDU
Reality Filter
for weaknesses**

IS IT DIFFICULT TO FIX?

Genuine weaknesses are attributes that cannot easily be corrected by the firm. For example, the brand may have some inherent limitation in efficacy or restriction in regulatory approval that requires medium to long term investment to correct. Attributes that could be modified in the short to medium term, such as temporary supply issues or weakness in the technical knowledge of sales teams, are not weaknesses, even if they meet the other three criteria for a weakness.

IS IT UNCOMPENSATED FOR BY OTHER FACTORS?

Genuine weaknesses are attributes that are not counteracted by some other part of the organisation's strategy, processes or other characteristics. For example, lack of a local medical science liaison presence might be considered irrelevant to customers of a generic drug company, where it is offset by low costs. The same would not be true of a high-cost, novel oncology brand. Attributes that are compensated for by other factors, as these examples show, are not weaknesses, even if they meet the other three criteria for a weakness.

Figure 6.3 *The MUDU Reality Filter for weaknesses*

Exercise 6.3

Gather together the putative opportunities developed from your application of other strategy tools and other sources. Test each against the four criteria for a valid opportunity. A strong answer will provide clear reasons for the removal of some putative opportunities and for the retention of a small number of validated opportunities. A weak answer will retain non-validated opportunities.

but, if it's common in your sector, then it's not an important weakness. Those weaknesses that meet all four criteria, your MUDU-validated weaknesses, are those that your brand must either correct or mitigate in the face of threats, as described in the SWOT Alignment process in Chapter 5.

Step 3: Which of our perceived opportunities are really opportunities?

As with the internal factors of strengths and weaknesses, testing external opportunities begins with a collated list of perceived opportunities gleaned from using other tools in the book or other sources. Each perceived opportunity is tested for validity using the four questions in Figure 6.4.

It's relatively easy to assess whether an opportunity meets these four criteria, and doing so is another way to pool the brand team's knowledge. As with strengths and weaknesses, an opportunity is not an opportunity unless it meets *all four* criteria. Many of the opportunities being suggested in wearable technology, for example, may be complementary, large, accessible or lasting, but very few meet all four criteria. Those opportunities that do are CLAL-validated opportunities; your brand must leverage its strength to exploit them, as described in the SWOT Alignment process in Chapter 5.

IS IT COMPLEMENTARY?

Genuine opportunities reinforce or at least do not conflict with other opportunities. For example, a possible target segment characterised by innovative payers, whose usage would positively influence another segment of mainstream payers, would be complementary. By contrast, if usage by a potential target segment would discourage use by other segments, it may conflict. For example, a segment characterised by a particular patient phenotype might create the idea that the brand is a restricted use, niche product. As these examples illustrate, opportunities that conflict with or do not reinforce other opportunities are not opportunities, even if they meet the other three criteria for an opportunity.

IS IT LARGE?

Genuine opportunities are sufficiently large to justify the costs of exploiting them. For example, an in vitro diagnostics company that was already successfully providing small, rapid results instruments to small hospital laboratories might judge that the community general practice segment, seeking point of care results, was large enough to justify the relatively small additional resources needed to exploit it. By contrast, that same company might judge that the potentially larger personal patient use segment was not large enough to justify the relatively very large resources needed to exploit that more consumer-like market. As these examples illustrate, opportunities that do not justify their exploitation are not opportunities, even if they meet the other three criteria for an opportunity.

CLAL Reality Filter for opportunities

IS IT ACCESSIBLE?

Genuine opportunities are practically accessible to the brand. For example, well established channels and recognised Rx brands mean that OTC medicine segments are relatively accessible to many pharma brands. By contrast, only the simplest medtech brands manage to make that switch because their brand recognition, channel constraints and regulatory constraints make many consumer segments inaccessible to technologically advanced medtech brands. As these examples illustrate, opportunities that are not accessible are not opportunities, even if they meet the other three criteria for an opportunity.

IS IT LASTING?

Genuine opportunities are durable enough to justify the effort and resources needed to exploit them. For example, segments in chronic diseases or associated with long term trends, such as the shift to more personalised medicines, can reasonably be expected to last many years and so be worth the effort needed to develop and execute brand strategies. By contrast, some segments in cosmetic surgery grow and dissipate in a matter of a year or two. As these examples illustrate, opportunities that are short lived are not opportunities, even if they meet the other three criteria for an opportunity.

Figure 6.4 *The CLAL Reality Filter for opportunities*

Step 4: Which of our perceived threats are really threats?

Exercise 6.4

Gather together the putative threats developed from your application of other strategy tools and other sources. Test each against the four criteria for a valid threat. A strong answer will provide clear reasons for both the removal of some putative threats and the retention of a small number of validated threats. A weak answer will retain non-validated threats.

As with the other factors, filtering external threats begins by collating a list of perceived threats from the other tools in the book or elsewhere. Then each perceived threat is tested for validity using the four questions in Figure 6.5.

Judging whether a putative threat meets these four criteria isn't usually difficult, and results in a valuable brand team discussion. As with strengths, weaknesses and opportunities, a threat is not a threat unless it meets *all four* criteria. For example, many of the threats being suggested by globalisation, whilst worth evaluating, may be unmitigated, significant, undefended against or lasting but not all four. Those threats that do meet all four criteria are classed as USUL-validated threats. These are the threats against which your brand must mitigate its weaknesses so as to prevent their exacerbation. This is described in Chapter 5.

IS IT UNMITIGATED?

Genuine threats are not mitigated by other external factors. For example, a small, speciality brand and a large volume primary care brand may each perceive the threat of buyer pressure (see Chapter 9). However, whilst that threat may be real for the latter, it is probably mitigated for the former by the buyers' strategy of focusing on large, easy savings. Equally, a threat of volume decline in, for example, lung cancer due to lifestyle changes in developed markets may be mitigated by the growth of the market in developing markets. As these examples illustrate, threats that are mitigated by other factors are not threats, even if they meet the other three criteria for a threat.

IS IT SIGNIFICANT?

Genuine threats are capable of having a significant impact on the brand. For example, the entrant of a strong new competitor whose innovative products compete across the whole market would be a genuine threat. The entrant of a fifth or sixth me-too competitor, with small resources, would not be. Equally, changes in clinical practice that obviate your brand would be much more significant than those that merely change how your product is used. As these examples illustrate, threats that do not have significant impact on the brand are not threats, even if they meet the other three criteria for a threat.

USUL Reality Filter for threats

IS IT UNDEFENDED?

Genuine threats are not already defended against by some existing activity. For example, long standing activities of direct competitors to denigrate your brand, to which defensive activity is already in place in sales training and marketing materials, are not a genuine threat. By contrast, the deployment by a direct competitor of some new clinical information with substantial evidence would be. As these examples illustrate, threats that are already defended against are not threats, even if they meet the other three criteria for a threat.

IS IT LASTING?

Genuine threats are sustained for a long enough period of time to have an impact on your brand. For example, the introduction of arbitrary price controls by government purchasers is a genuine threat, whilst a short-term price-reduction tactic by a competitor is unlikely to be. The same is true of new market entrants, which are lasting, and most competitor marketing campaigns, which are not. As these examples illustrate, threats that are short lived are not threats, even if they meet the other three criteria for a threat.

Figure 6.5 *The USUL Reality Filter for threats*

What should I do with the filtered information?

The output of using the Reality Filters tool is a list of validated strengths, weaknesses, opportunities and threats, similar to that shown in Table 5.3 for SWOT Alignment (Chapter 5). The numbers will vary, but good brand strategies usually identify between ten and fifteen of each of the four factors at this stage. These form the inputs into the SWOT Alignment tool. Applying the SWOT Alignment tool combines them and the number is usually reduced to five to ten of each. As well as being the inputs into the SWOT Alignment, these factors also have an important use in communicating within and beyond the brand team. As a succinct, and therefore easily communicated, summary of the really important issues, a list of validated strengths, weaknesses, opportunities and threats is extremely useful when creating the brand strategy. It allows the brand team to build a clear, shared view of their situation and to ensure that their colleagues also understand what's going on in the market. As such, it's much more useful and powerful than the over-long, ill-thought-out slide decks that unsuccessfully fill that role in many pharma and medtech companies.

Pragmatic advice for brand leaders

The purpose of the Reality Filters is to correct perceptions of the situation that are the false creations of our imperfect human cognition. They take what we believe and turn it into reality. This is a politically dangerous thing to do in any organisation. False perceptions of strengths, weaknesses, opportunities and threats survive because they benefit someone or other. For example, a belief that our sales people are better than the industry average serves the interests of sales leadership. A belief that our marketing budget is relatively small serves the interests of marketing leaders lobbying for an increase.

A mirage-like opportunity that a certain segment or geography is worth exploiting favours the person who will be given resources and prestige to attack it. An espoused threat is an excellent excuse for under-performance. All of this means that, when developing and communicating a list of validated strengths, weaknesses, opportunities and threats, the brand leader needs to allow for political sensitivities. This means involving those whose interests might be damaged and bringing them along where possible. Where it is not, senior leadership need to be convinced of the reality of the situation. The situation to avoid, which occurs frequently, is one in which vested political interests end up diluting or replacing a rigorously developed and validated view of reality so that you end up with a politically-acceptable, consensus view that is detached from reality.

Strong brand strategies are focused: Using the Focus Matrix to guide complex strategies

In complex markets, strong brand strategies make nuanced choices about how much and what kind of resource each target segment needs. This chapter describes how to make those choices to achieve optimal return on investment.

When should I use the Focus Matrix?

The Focus Matrix is one of two tools (the other being SWOT Alignment) that process the outputs of other strategic tools and then strongly directs your choice of brand strategy. Its most important inputs are the outputs of the Contextual Segmentation tool (Chapter 10), but it is also uses ideas developed from the other tools in this book. The output of the Focus Matrix is a recommendation for the broad strategic approach to each segment. Figure 7.1 shows where the Focus Matrix fits into the brand strategy process.

Figure 7.1 *Where the Focus Matrix fits into the brand strategy process*

Why is the Focus Matrix especially important in pharma and medtech markets?

Two peculiarities of pharma and medtech markets make the Focus Matrix particularly important.
 ↪ diverse
The first is the increasing heterogeneity of each market, as described in Chapter 10, due to the involvement of professionals, payers and patients in brand choice. This means that there are likely to be many contextual segments in each market and, to achieve commercial goals, brand strategy will often have to win several of those segments. But variation between the needs of different segments also means that they vary in what it takes to win them and what returns they will provide. If resources were spread evenly across this heterogeneous market, some segments would get too much and others would get too little. In both cases, this would result in a sub-optimal return on investment. In other words, a complex, heterogeneous market requires the nuanced focusing of resources.

The second distinctive characteristic of pharma and medtech is that allocation of resources between segments is largely controlled by commercial leaders who spent their formative years in sales. Sales team culture values determination and a refusal to give up in the face of reluctant customers. This culture is beneficial in a front-line sales context but, like all cultures, has a downside too. People who learned their values in sales teams often want to pursue every customer and are reluctant to limit effort in any way. This can lead to a culturally embedded tendency to prioritise everyone and, in so doing, spread resources evenly and without focus.

These two factors—a market that demands focus and a culture that resists it—are why the Focus Matrix is especially important in pharma and medtech.

What is the Focus Matrix and how does it work?

The Focus Matrix is a method of deciding for each segment how much and what kind of resource is appropriate. It does this by asking two questions:

- How attractive to us is each segment, relative to the other segments?
- How attractive to each segment is our brand, relative to our competitors?

The answers to these questions allow you to put each segment into a matrix. The resulting positions in that matrix dictate how much resource, and of what kind, each segment should receive for optimal return on investment. This is illustrated in Figure 7.2.

The principle of a Focus Matrix is quite simple, but its practice involves careful thought, which provides another opportunity for the brand team to develop a deep, shared understanding of the market. Firms that have mastered this tool break down its execution into five steps:

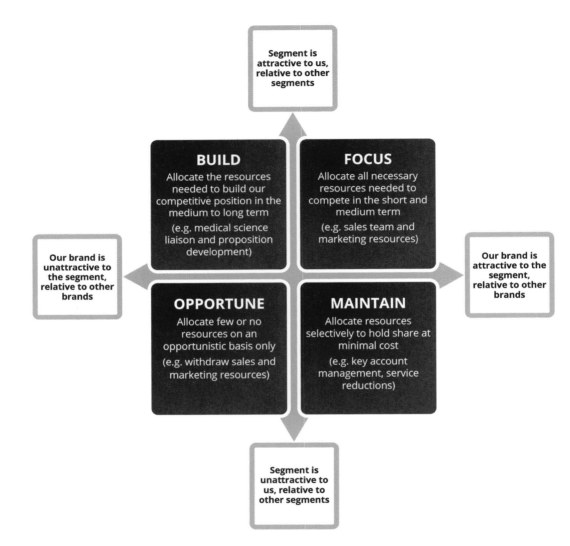

Figure 7.2 *The concept of the Focus Matrix*

Step 1: What contextual segments do we need to allocate resources between?

Using a Focus Matrix begins with collating the outputs of the Contextual Segmentation analysis (Chapter 10). This will typically be five to ten contextual segments, between which your brand strategy must allocate resources. The Focus Matrix will not work if categories, such as disease states or product categories, are input into the matrix. That is because categories, unlike contextual segments, are heterogeneous in both their attractiveness to us and our ability to meet their needs.

Step 2: What determines the relative attractiveness of each segment?

The second step is to decide what makes a segment attractive to your brand. Unskilled brand teams default to a 'bigger is better' position but there are several things in addition to size that make a segment attractive, for example:

- the volume product usage of the segment
- the profit available in the segment

Exercise 7.1

Using the results of the exercises in Chapter 10, list the contextual segments in your market. Strong answers will comprise around five to ten contextual segments, in each of which brand choice is driven by a characteristic set of motivating needs. Weak answers will confuse contextual segments with heterogeneous customer or product categories.

Exercise 7.2

Using Table 7.1 as a guide, estimate and weight the factors that make a segment attractive to you. Strong answers will identify about four factors and weight them according to their influence on ROI. Weak answers will identity many factors and weight them without reference to ROI impact.

83

- the influence this segment has on other segments, also known as external synergy
- the influence this segment has on the effectiveness or efficiency of internal processes, also known as internal synergy
- the rate of change of any of the above, and
- the stability or cyclicity of the segment.

Bear in mind that although these attractiveness factors are characteristics of the segment, their relative importance depends on the company's ROI goals. The brand team's task is to choose which factors to consider and to weight each one as shown in the example (Table 7.1). Note that the weightings come to a total of 100.

Table 7.1 *Weighting of segment attractiveness factors*

ATTRACTIVENESS FACTOR	WEIGHTING/100	REASON FOR WEIGHTING
Volume product usage of the segment	10	Our ROI goals are not influenced much by the volume of the product we sell.
Profit available in the segment	50	Our ROI goals depend heavily on achieving a high gross margin.
Influence this segment has on other segments	30	Our ROI goals depend on winning significant share of several segments in this market.
Stability or cyclicity of the segment	10	Our ROI goals are not influenced significantly by variation of volume over time.
Total (=100)	100	

Step 3: What is the relative attractiveness of each segment?

The third step in the process is to use the weighted factors from Step 2 to assess the relative attractiveness of each segment, as shown in the example in Table 7.2.

Table 7.2 *Example of segment attractiveness calculation*

ATTRACTIVENESS FACTOR	WEIGHTING/100	CONTEXTUAL SEGMENT A	CONTEXTUAL SEGMENT B	CONTEXTUAL SEGMENT C	CONTEXTUAL SEGMENT D
Volume product usage of the segment	10	10	9	3	1
Profit available in the segment	50	7	9	3	2
Influence this segment has on other segments	30	6	8	4	1
Stability or cyclicity of the segment	10	5	5	5	5
Aggregate relative attractiveness	(Total = 100)	10x10 =100 50x7 = 350 30x6 = 180 10x5 = 50 Total = 680	10x9 = 90 50x9 = 450 30x8 = 240 10x5 = 50 Total = 830	10x3 = 30 50x3 = 150 30x4 = 120 10x5 = 50 Total = 350	10x1 = 10 50x2 = 100 30x1 = 30 10x5 = 50 Total = 190

The skill in completing this step is to recognise that segment attractiveness is relative, not absolute. The *most* attractive segment must be 8, 9 or 10, the *least* must be 1, 2 or

3, with moderately attractive segments between these extremes. Within this, the assessments are relative based on what you know about the segment. In this example, there is little difference in volume usage between A and B. Equally, B is clearly much more influential than C. When the segments don't differ on an attractiveness factor, they all should be assessed as 5, as with stability in our example. Once these relative assessments of the attractiveness of each segment have been made against each attractiveness factor, the aggregate relative attractiveness is calculated as shown.

Step 4: What determines the relative attractiveness of a brand to each segment?

The fourth step is to decide what makes a brand attractive to each segment. This varies between segments, so the weighting of each factor is different for each segment. See the example in Table 7.3. Note that the weightings come to a total of 100.

Note that these attractiveness factors and their weightings are characteristics of the segment. The brand team's task, based on the needs that define the segment, is to accurately judge which factors, at what weights, accurately describe the motivations of each contextual segment. In this example, Segment D is controlled by price-driven payers whilst professionals' and patients' needs are secondary. Segment A is driven by value-seeking payers whilst B and C are driven by professionals' clinical motivations.

Table 7.3 *Weighting of brand attractiveness factors by contextual segment*

ATTRACTIVENESS FACTOR	WEIGHTING FOR CONTEXTUAL SEGMENT A	WEIGHTING FOR CONTEXTUAL SEGMENT B	WEIGHTING FOR CONTEXTUAL SEGMENT C	WEIGHTING FOR CONTEXTUAL SEGMENT D
Unit price	10	20	5	70
Level of health economic evidence	55	5	5	10
Contraindication and side effects	10	65	85	10
Extent of use by other healthcare systems	25	10	5	10
Total (=100)	100	100	100	100

Step 5: What is our brand's relative attractiveness to each segment?

The fifth step is to use the factors from Step 4 to assess your brand's attractiveness to each segment, relative to your competitors. This is done in two stages. Firstly, we assess your brand's competitive strength on each attractiveness factor, as in Table 7.4, in which the highest number implies the highest competitive strength (e.g. lowest price, best contraindication or side effect profile).

Table 7.4 *Relative competitive strength of your brand by factor*

ATTRACTIVENESS FACTOR	OUR BRAND	COMPETITOR 1	COMPETITOR 2	COMPETITOR 3
Unit price	2	3	7	9
Level of health economic evidence	2	4	8	6
Contraindication and side effects	10	7	4	1
Extent of use by other healthcare systems	1	3	8	7

Exercise 7.5

Using Table 7.4 as a guide, and the results of Exercise 7.4, estimate the relative competitive strength of your brand and its main competitors for each attractiveness factor. Strong answers will clearly differentiate between brands based on market evidence. Weak answers will see little difference between competitors and will not use market evidence.

The second stage is to assess our relative attractiveness to each segment, allowing for their different weighting for each factor. An example of this calculation is shown in Table 7.5.

The skill in completing this step is to recognise that your brand's attractiveness varies with the differing drivers of each segment. In this example, the price motivation of Segment D makes your brand less attractive to them than your competitors. By contrast, your clinical performance makes you more attractive to Segment C than competitors with poorer performance. Your overall attractiveness to each contextual segment is the weighted aggregate of the four different attractiveness factors.

Table 7.5 *Relative competitive strength of your brand by contextual segment*

ATTRACTIVENESS FACTOR	RELATIVE COMPETITIVE STRENGTH IN CONTEXTUAL SEGMENT A	RELATIVE COMPETITIVE STRENGTH IN CONTEXTUAL SEGMENT B	RELATIVE COMPETITIVE STRENGTH IN CONTEXTUAL SEGMENT C	RELATIVE COMPETITIVE STRENGTH IN CONTEXTUAL SEGMENT D
Unit price	10x2	20x2	5x2	70x2
Level of health economic evidence	55x2	5x2	5x2	10x2
Contraindication and side effects	10x10	65x10	85x10	10x10
Extent of use by other healthcare systems	25x1	10x1	5x1	10x1
Total	10x2 = 20 55x2 = 110 10x10 = 100 25x1 = 25 Total = 255	20x2 = 40 5x2 = 10 65x10 = 650 10x1 = 10 Total = 710	5x2 = 10 5x2 = 10 85x10 = 850 5x1 = 5 Total = 875	70x2 = 140 10x2 = 20 10x10 = 100 10x1 = 10 Total = 270

Step 6: What do these relative attractiveness assessments imply for brand strategy?

Steps 4 and 5, when completed, provide quantified judgements of two values for each segment, as shown in Table 7.6. These are used to populate the Focus Matrix, as shown in Figure 7.3.

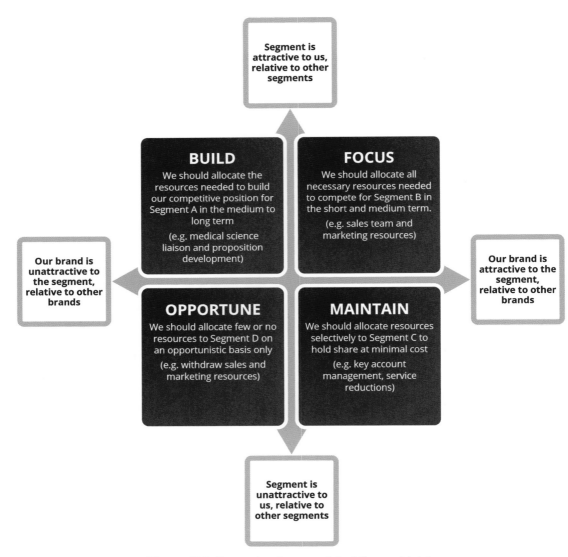

Figure 7.3 *Example of a populated Focus Matrix*

Table 7.6 *Focus grid assessments*

	RELATIVE SEGMENT ATTRACTIVENESS TO US	RELATIVE COMPETITIVE STRENGTH OF OUR BRAND IN THIS SEGMENT
Contextual Segment A	680	255
Contextual Segment B	830	710
Contextual Segment C	350	875
Contextual Segment D	190	270

The populated matrix provides broad strategic guidance for what to do with each segment. In addition, it also provides a more detailed level of guidance based on what might be changed for each segment, as shown in Table 7.7.

Table 7.7 *Example of guidance from the Focus Matrix*

	OBSERVATIONS	IMPLIED STRATEGIC GUIDANCE
Contextual Segment A	We are currently unable to compete effectively in Segment A only because we cannot currently address their need for health economic evidence.	Direct sales and marketing effort would be wasted on Segment A. We should allocate resources to developing the necessary market access strategy.
Contextual Segment B	We can compete strongly in Segment B as we meet their needs better than any competitor.	We should focus sales and marketing effort onto Segment B with an emphasis on our side effect profile.

	OBSERVATIONS	IMPLIED STRATEGIC GUIDANCE
Contextual Segment C	Segment C has little alternative to our brand but consumes many resources for little return.	We should selectively withdraw resources from Segment C where this will not affect share.
Contextual Segment D	We will never be able to meet Segment D's need for lowest possible price and they are disinterested in non-price benefits.	We should divert resources from Segment D to Segment B, serving Segment D only if circumstances allow profitable business.

Exercise 7.6

Using Table 7.5 as a guide, and the results of Exercises 7.4 and 7.5, estimate the relative competitive strength of your brand by contextual segment. Strong answers will clearly differentiate between brands based on market evidence. Weak answers will see little difference between competitors and not use market evidence.

What should I do with my Focus Matrix results?

If all six steps are completed carefully, and assuming the inputs are well-defined contextual segments, then the result of the Focus Matrix is a list of brand strategy recommendations as shown in Table 7.7. Along with the outputs of the SWOT Alignment, these recommendations feed into the development of your brand strategy statement (Chapter 3). Of equal importance, the Focus Matrix process helps develop a shared view amongst the brand team about what are the really salient issues in the market and how your brand competes in it. In almost all cases, this knowledge makes the brand strategy decision quite clear. It is often said that one doesn't decide a strategy, one merely uncovers what it must be. The Focus Matrix is, along with the SWOT Alignment, one of the most powerful tools for uncovering your brand strategy.

Pragmatic advice for brand leaders

The Focus Matrix is a powerful technique for guiding strategies that involve multiple segments. Its fundamental logic is very simple (focus on where you can win that which is worth winning) and difficult to argue with. The detail of the process captures the specifics of each case and builds shared understanding. In practice, the Focus Matrix faces two challenges of implementation. The first is that it only works if your input segments are well defined. This is often problematic. Weak segmentation (e.g. categorisation) is often culturally embedded in pharma and medtech companies and changing it requires fresh thinking and significant effort, both of which may elicit a negative response. You will meet the usual range of reactions to change—it's too difficult, there's no proof it will work, we don't have time—and it is the job of the brand leader to overcome these. The second challenge will occur only when you have seen the results of using this tool. It will guide you to put more resources into focus segments and few will argue with that. However, it will also tell you to limit the resources put into segments in the build, maintain and opportune parts of the matrix. To the extent that those changes in resource allocation threaten vested interests, political power and long-standing habits, you should expect resistance. Again, it is the job of the brand leader to overcome this.

Strong brand strategies are your own: Using Value Chain Comparison to identify your firm's distinctive strengths and weaknesses

Strong brand strategies leverage distinctive strengths, whilst either correcting or mitigating significant weaknesses. This chapter guides you to uncover and understand what your firm's characteristic strengths and weaknesses really are.

When should I use Value Chain Comparison?

Value Chain Comparison identifies your firm's strengths and weaknesses with consideration for their relevance to the market, so it is used after you have developed a Customer-Centric Market Definition (Chapter 2). It provides, via the VRIO and MUDU Reality Filters (Chapter 6), the internal strength and weakness inputs into the SWOT Alignment (Chapter 5) that align to the external opportunities and threats provided by the other tools. The place of Value Chain Comparison in the brand strategy process is shown in Figure 8.1.

Figure 8.1 *Where Value Chain Comparison fits in the brand strategy process*

Why is Value Chain Comparison especially important in pharma and medtech markets?

Because of their scientific heritage, pharma and medtech companies have two cultural characteristics that, whilst not unique to the industry, are more strongly embedded here than in other sectors. The first is product-orientation; most pharma and medtech firms see their market as a competition between products. The second is specialisation; pharma and medtech companies are structured as collections of very specialised functions that work together across cross-functional boundaries. These two cultural characteristics have advantages. For example, it enables firms to perform the large number of very complex tasks that are needed to invent, make and bring to market new medicines and medical technology. However, like all cultural traits, they have some downsides.

One important downside of our industry's product-oriented, specialised culture is that it's difficult to identify a firm's strengths and weaknesses. A first estimate of these for any brand typically identifies few factors that survive the Reality Filters (Chapter 6). This is because a product-oriented, specialised culture makes it hard to see non-product strengths and weaknesses across the whole organisation. That is what the Value Chain Comparison tool does.

So, our product-oriented and specialised culture risks blinding us to our own strengths and weaknesses. That is why the Value Chain Comparison tool is especially useful in pharma and medtech.

What is Value Chain Comparison and how does it work?

A value chain is the entire sequence of activities needed to bring a product to market—from early research through development, manufacturing and operations to customer-facing activities. Value Chain Comparison is built on two simple ideas. Firstly, it's not brands but value chains that compete with each other. Secondly, brand strategies are only effective when the choice of target segments and offers make best use of your value chain's advantages and minimises its disadvantages. The Value Chain Comparison tool works by deconstructing the value chain into several value-creating stages and probing for evidence of relative strengths and weaknesses in each stage. This forces the brand team to think beyond the product and across functional boundaries. A move away from thinking about the product towards thinking about the value chain is not an easy transition. Brand teams that have mastered the craft of the Value Chain Comparison execute it in a series of six steps:

Step 1: What are the value-creating activities in our value chain?

The first step in Value Chain Comparison is to define the activities in your value chain that could be the sources of your strengths and weaknesses. Every value chain in pharma and medtech is similar, in that it involves three core stages, supported by four sets of organisational activity, as shown in Figure 8.2.

Human resources, including resource planning, organisational development and compliance with employment law

Infrastructure, including information systems and other facilities management

NEW PRODUCT DEVELOPMENT

Including basic research and discovery, in-licensing, all stages of development and regulatory approval of new products

SUPPLY CHAIN MANAGEMENT

Including procurement of materials, manufacturing and logistics (inbound and outbound) and compliance with manufacturing regulation

CUSTOMER RELATIONSHIP MANAGEMENT

Including market access, medical affairs, sales and marketing and compliance with marketing regulation

Legal, including commercial law and compliance with local, national and global legislation

Finance, including treasury functions, financial controls and compliance with financial regulation

Figure 8.2 *Generalised Value Chain for pharma and medtech*

Although similar at this generalised level, value chains differ greatly both between firms and between brands within firms. There are two main variations:

- *How much of each activity is done*
  For example, more discovery and development activity is done in a research-led company than in a market-follower company. Similarly, some companies provide only basic support for their product whilst, for others, value-adding services are a large component of their offer.

- *How much of the activity is done inside the firm or by external partners*

  Most pharma and medtech firms outsource some parts of the value chain in New Product Development (NPD), e.g. by in-licensing, Supply Chain Management (SCM), e.g. by contract manufacturing, and Customer Relationship Management (CRM), e.g. by contract sales forces or out-licensing; but the extent of this varies greatly. Some firms outsource only the most basic activities, others keep only the most important activities in house.

Because value chains vary so much, identifying your brand's characteristic strengths and weaknesses must start with defining the major activities of your brand's value chain. Somewhere in this list lie both your relative strengths and your relative weaknesses.

Step 2: What are our strengths and weaknesses in New Product Development?

Exercise 8.1

Using Figure 8.2 as a guide, map out the value chain activities for your brand. For each part of the value chain, identify the principal activities that create value but exclude those routine activities that are merely necessary to operations. A good answer will identify 30 to 50 activities, performed either within the firm or by partners, that are important to your brand's ability to compete. These activities will usually reflect the nature of your company's strategy (e.g. research-based or low-cost follower). A weak answer will omit important competitive activities, include routine activities or will not reflect the strategy of the firm.

The second step of Value Chain Comparison is to consider those activities in the NPD stage and look for evidence of relative advantages or disadvantages that arise from each one. These may be explicit, technological features in the product, such as efficacy or ease

Exercise 8.2

Using the NPD value chain activities you identified in Exercise 8.1, list what strengths and weaknesses your brand may have that arise from NPD activity. A good answer will consider all the NPD activities identified in your value chain and will identify both explicit and implicit strengths and weaknesses. A weak answer will omit important activities, strengths and weaknesses.

Exercise 8.3

Using the SCM value chain activities you identified in Exercise 8.1, list the strengths and weaknesses your brand may have that arise from SCM activity. A good answer will consider all the SCM activities identified in your value chain and identify both explicit and implicit strengths and weaknesses. A weak answer will omit important activities, strengths and weaknesses.

of use. Or they may be implicit, such as capabilities in generating clinical evidence, relationships with scientific opinion leaders or a trustworthy reputation in particular disease or technology areas. Whether explicit or implicit, these are the result of the NPD part of your brand's value chain that you believe to be stronger or weaker than the competition.

Step 3: What are our strengths and weaknesses in Supply Chain Management?

The third step in Value Chain Comparison is to consider those activities in the SCM stage and look for evidence of relative advantage or disadvantage that arise from each one. Again, these may be explicit, such as proprietary features of the manufacturing process or dedicated logistics channels. Or they may be implicit, such as capabilities in flexible manufacturing, relationships with key suppliers or a strong reputation for product quality or continuity of supply. Whether explicit or implicit, these are the result of the SCM part of your brand's value chain that you believe to be stronger or weaker than the competition.

Step 4: What are our strengths and weaknesses in Customer Relationship Management?

The fourth step in Value Chain Comparison is to consider those activities in the CRM stage and look for evidence of relative advantage or disadvantage that arise from each activity. Explicit examples might include brand recognition or sales and marketing capabilities. Implicit examples would be relationships with key opinion leaders or capabilities to deliver added value services. Whether explicit or implicit, these are the result of the CRM part of your brand's value chain that you believe to be stronger or weaker than the competition.

Step 5: What are our other organisational strengths and weaknesses?

The fifth step in Value Chain Comparison is to look for evidence of relative advantages or disadvantages that arise from those activities in the organisation that support NPD, SCM and CRM. Explicit examples might include corporate brand recognition

Exercise 8.4

Using the CRM value chain activities you identified in Exercise 8.1, list the strengths and weaknesses your brand may have that arise from CRM activity. A good answer will consider all the CRM activities identified in your value chain and will identify both explicit and implicit strengths and weaknesses. A weak answer will omit important activities, strengths and weaknesses.

Exercise 8.5

Using the value chain activities in human resources, finance, legal and infrastructure you identified in Exercise 8.1 as a guide, list the strengths and weaknesses your brand may have that arise from supporting activity. A good answer will consider all the supporting activities identified in your value chain and will identify both explicit and implicit strengths and weaknesses. A weak answer will omit important activities, strengths and weaknesses.

101

or human resource capabilities shared with other brands in the firm's range. Implicit examples would include relationships with government or regulatory bodies and partnerships with other firms. Whether explicit or implicit, these are the result of the supporting parts of your brand's value chain that you believe to be stronger or weaker than the competition.

Exercise 8.6

Using the results of Exercises 8.2 to 8.5, collate all your putative strengths and weaknesses. Strong answers will include strengths and weaknesses across the entire value chain. Weak answers will omit important activities, strengths and weaknesses.

Step 6: How does our value chain compare?

The final stage in Value Chain Comparison is to collate the putative strengths and weaknesses across your entire value chain. Typically, this results in a list of ten to twenty putative strengths and weaknesses whose distribution is usually uneven across the value chain and is a reflection of the firm's core strategy and heritage.

What should I do with my Value Chain Comparison?

Whilst various strategic tools feed external opportunities and threats into the Reality Filters, Value Chain Comparison is the primary tool for identifying internal strengths and weaknesses. Its outputs feed into the VRIO and MUDU Reality Filters (Chapter 6), which then feed into the SWOT Alignment (Chapter 5). As such, Value Chain Comparison is a valuable, often underused tool that is essential to the brand strategy process.

Pragmatic advice for brand leaders

Many of the tools described in this book are already used, nominally at least, by brand teams. The issue with, for example, SWOT and segmentation is not the failure to use them, but that they are used badly. Value Chain Comparison is different. It is rarely used in any form. Strengths and weaknesses, where they are considered, are usually extracted from product features and benefits materials used by sales teams. This approach commits sins of omission (it misses important factors) and commission (it includes things that are neither strengths nor weaknesses). This makes the use of Value Chain Comparison both important and difficult. Two practical difficulties frequently emerge. The first is that this tool requires brand teams to think deeply about things they don't usually consider—such as the value created by the supply chain—and to think far beyond the product. Both requirements are difficult and will therefore generate resistance. Brand team members may downplay the importance of non-product strengths and weaknesses or claim they don't have the information to know these things. It is the job of the brand leader to overcome this resistance. The second difficulty is that, even after applying Value Chain Comparison well, the brand team may still struggle to identify important strengths and weaknesses. In this case, it's a good idea to supplement Value Chain Comparison with the Hypothesis Loop (Chapter 13). Look for different contexts in which the brand has been successful or has failed and try to develop and test hypotheses to explain these events. Using the Hypothesis Loop often reveals strengths and weaknesses that haven't been previously considered.

Strong brand strategies overcome the competition: Using Competitive Pressure Analysis to identify competitive threats and opportunities

Strong brand strategies understand what creates competitive pressures and how they are likely to change. This chapter explains how you can use the characteristics of your market to anticipate and respond to your wider competitive environment.

When should I use Competitive Pressure Analysis?

Competitive Pressure Analysis is important in all pharma and medtech markets but especially in the most mature ones, where competitive intensity is at its highest. It can only be used once the market has been defined in customer-centric terms (Chapter 1). It's one of the tools that examines the external environment, and its opportunity and threat outputs become the inputs of SWOT Alignment (Chapter 5), after validation by the CLAL and USUL Reality Filters (Chapter 6). The place of Competitive Pressure Analysis in the brand strategy process is shown in Figure 9.1.

Figure 9.1 *Where Competitive Pressure Analysis fits into the brand strategy process*

Why is Competitive Pressure Analysis especially important in pharma and medtech markets?

Brand planning in any market must take account of competitive pressures in order to defend against them. It's especially important in pharma and medtech markets for two reasons.

The first is that pharma and medtech are capital intensive industries with lots of investment required in fixed costs such as research, manufacturing and distribution. Capital intensive firms need high margins in order to achieve even an average ROI. This accounting reality makes it essential that brand strategies in pharma and medtech understand and allow for competitive pressures on their profits, not just their sales. That's the first fundamental difference between Competitive Pressure Analysis and other competitive analysis techniques.

The second is the industry's product-oriented culture. This leads to many brand teams equating competition with other, similar products. But pharma and medtech are distress markets, meaning the customer is trying to solve a problem and would be very happy to buy something other than a medicine or a device if it solved the same problem for less cost. This means that we must consider competitive pressures from all directions, not just direct rivals. That's a second fundamental difference between Competitive Pressure Analysis and other competitive analysis techniques.

For these two reasons—capital intensity requiring profitability, and distress needs creating indirect competition—Competitive Pressure Analysis is especially important in pharma and medtech.

What is Competitive Pressure Analysis and how does it work?

Competitive Pressure Analysis is a method for identifying the threats to the profitability of your brand and suggesting responses to alleviate those pressures. It works by recognising that there are five sources of competitive pressure and that each is increased or decreased under different market conditions. By considering the market conditions of your brand, it anticipates the opportunities and threats that arise from the competitive environment. Those firms that use it effectively do so using six steps.

Exercise 9.1

Consider the conditions shown in Figure 9.2 and how they are expected to change in your market. How likely is direct rivalry to change and in what direction? Strong answers will consider all market conditions and anticipate the likely degree and direction of change, as well as the nature of the threat or opportunity (e.g. price competition or reduced competitor-sales activity). Weak answers will ignore some conditions and won't fully anticipate either the change in competitive pressure from direct rivals or the form it will take.

Step 1: How much direct rivalry will there be?

The most obvious competitive pressure on profitability is direct competition from other pharma and medtech companies. This pressure occurs when customers have similar alternatives to which they can switch relatively easily. This leads to price competition and margin erosion. Like all competitive pressures, direct competition is encouraged by some market conditions and reduced by others. These opposing forces are shown in Figure 9.2.

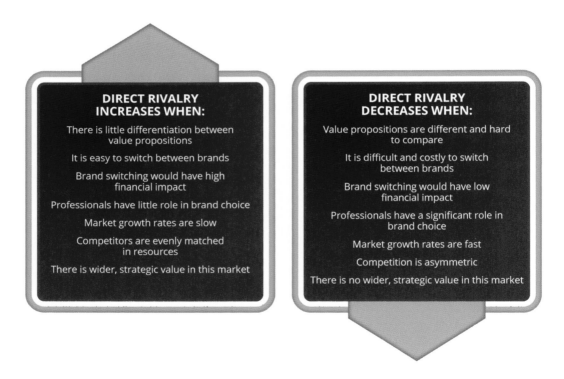

DIRECT RIVALRY INCREASES WHEN:

There is little differentiation between value propositions

It is easy to switch between brands

Brand switching would have high financial impact

Professionals have little role in brand choice

Market growth rates are slow

Competitors are evenly matched in resources

There is wider, strategic value in this market

DIRECT RIVALRY DECREASES WHEN:

Value propositions are different and hard to compare

It is difficult and costly to switch between brands

Brand switching would have low financial impact

Professionals have a significant role in brand choice

Market growth rates are fast

Competition is asymmetric

There is no wider, strategic value in this market

Figure 9.2 *Market conditions that increase or decrease direct rivalry*

By anticipating how the balance of these forces will change in the future, you can anticipate the increase or decrease of direct rivalry in your market. In pharma and medtech, direct competition tends to increase over time and in uneven steps, as exclusivity, from either intellectual property rights or technological barriers, is eroded. In pharma, the most extreme example is the patent-cliff and subsequent genericisation, whilst in medtech, direct competition tends to happen sooner but more gradually. Increasing direct rivalry usually creates two kinds of threat: price competition and increased sales and marketing activity by competitors. It's less common for direct rivalry to decrease but when this does happen, for instance, when a major competitor pulls out of the market, it provides an opportunity to increase profitability either by increasing prices or reducing sales and marketing costs.

Step 2: How much buyer pressure will there be?

Closely related to direct rivalry is the pressure your customers put on your profitability. This pressure also occurs when they have alternatives to which they can switch relatively easily. This leads to pressure on pricing via commoditisation. Buyer pressure is encouraged by some market conditions and reduced by others. These opposing forces are shown in Figure 9.3.

In pharma and medtech, buyer pressure is usually driven by payers, although the mechanism (price controls, tenders, contracts, risk sharing) varies according to situation. Naturally, the

Exercise 9.2

Consider the conditions shown in Figure 9.3 and how they are expected to change in your market. How likely is buyer pressure to change and in what direction? Strong answers will consider all market conditions and anticipate both the likely degree and direction of change, as well as the nature of the threat or opportunity (e.g. price controls or opportunity to increase prices). Weak answers will ignore some conditions and not fully anticipate either the change in buyer pressure or the form it will take.

109

most extreme buyer pressure comes in single-payer systems and for generic products. Increasing buyer pressure usually creates two kinds of threat: demands for lower prices and demands for increased value of some kind (service, payment terms etc.). It's less common for buyer pressure to decrease, but when this does happen (for example, when you're able to significantly differentiate your product), it provides an opportunity to increase profitability either by increasing prices, changing terms or reducing sales and marketing costs.

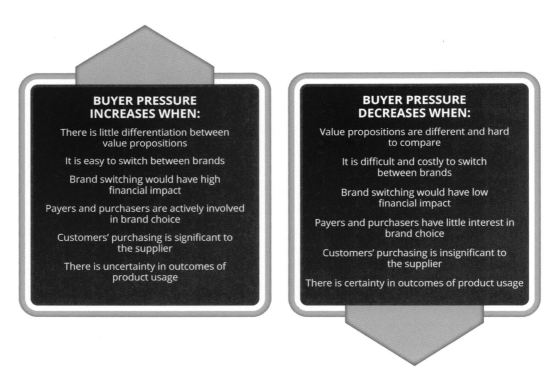

BUYER PRESSURE INCREASES WHEN:

There is little differentiation between value propositions

It is easy to switch between brands

Brand switching would have high financial impact

Payers and purchasers are actively involved in brand choice

Customers' purchasing is significant to the supplier

There is uncertainty in outcomes of product usage

BUYER PRESSURE DECREASES WHEN:

Value propositions are different and hard to compare

It is difficult and costly to switch between brands

Brand switching would have low financial impact

Payers and purchasers have little interest in brand choice

Customers' purchasing is insignificant to the supplier

There is certainty in outcomes of product usage

Figure 9.3 *Market conditions that increase or decrease buyer pressure*

Step 3: How much supplier pressure will there be?

Supplier pressure is less common but can seriously impact on your brand's profitability. It occurs when your brand's offer depends on one critical, non-substitutable input. This limits your ability to compete, or allows the supplier to increase their price, so reducing your brand's profitability. Supplier pressure is encouraged by certain market conditions and reduced in the absence of these conditions. These opposing forces are shown in Figure 9.4.

In pharma and medtech, supplier pressure rarely comes from a conventional supplier of raw materials and is often from some kind of intellectual property. The cost of in-licensed products or technologies is the clearest example, but so are specialist suppliers of critical components or services. Unique local distributors are an example of this. A special case of supplier pressure is when key people—specialist employees, partners such as academics or clinical trial centres—are difficult to source and threaten to make it impossible to deliver your offer. Increasing supplier pressure can therefore create two threats: the erosion of profit from increased costs and the prevention of sales because of constrained capabilities. Supplier pressure decreases when new suppliers or substitutes for them become available, creating opportunities to reduce costs or increase capabilities.

Exercise 9.3

Consider the conditions shown in Figure 9.4 and how they are expected to change in your market. How likely is supplier pressure to change and in what direction? Strong answers will consider all market conditions and anticipate both the likely degree and direction of change and the nature of the threat or opportunity (e.g. cost increases, limitations to supply or opportunity to decrease costs). Weak answers will ignore some conditions and not fully anticipate either the change in supplier pressure or the form it will take.

111

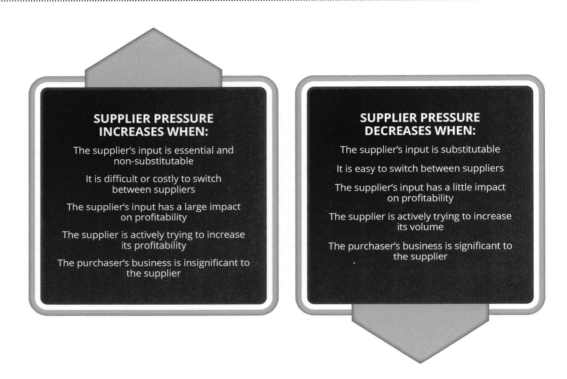

Figure 9.4 *Market conditions that increase or decrease supplier pressure*

Step 4: How much new entrant pressure will there be?

New entrant pressure is the slightly misleading term for when new capital is invested into your market. This usually takes the form of an acquisition of an existing competitor, the reinvigoration of a competitor by investment from its corporate owners, or the entrance of a pharma or medtech company from another disease area. Wholly new entrants are rare and usually take the form of substitutes (see Step 5). Whatever the source of new capital, the investors' need for it to create a satisfactory ROI will lead to some change in competitive intensity and threat to profitability. New entrants are encouraged by a particular set of market conditions and discouraged by the absence of these conditions. These opposing forces are shown in Figure 9.5.

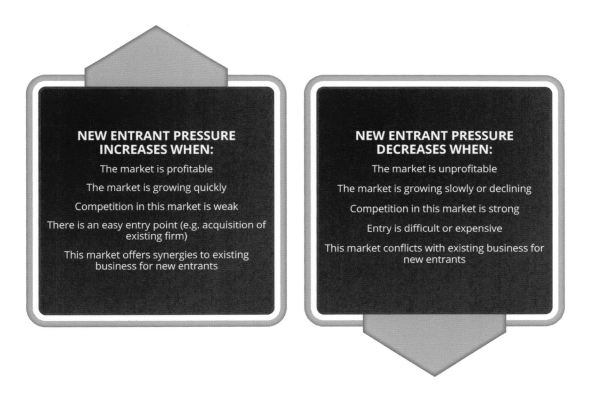

Figure 9.5 *Market conditions that increase or decrease new entrant pressure*

In pharma and medtech, technological and other barriers to entry mean that truly new entrants are rare, but industry consolidation and restructuring of large players often create opportunities for new injections of capital. Increasing new entrant pressure can create many kinds of threats, from increased marketing activity to an improved competitive

Exercise 9.4

Consider the conditions shown in Figure 9.5 and how they are expected to change in your market. How likely is new entrant pressure to change and in what direction? Strong answers will consider all market conditions and anticipate both the likely degree and direction of change and the nature of the threat or opportunity (e.g. invigorated competitors or opportunity to reduce costs). Weak answers will ignore some conditions and not fully anticipate either the change in competitive pressure from new entrants or the form it will take.

Exercise 9.5

Consider the conditions shown in Figure 9.6 and how they are expected to change in your market. How likely is substitute pressure to change and in what direction? Strong answers will consider all market conditions and anticipate both the likely degree and direction of change and the nature of the threat or opportunity (e.g. reduced category size or opportunity to grow sales). Weak answers will ignore some conditions and won't fully anticipate either the change in substitute pressure or the form it will take.

offer. The opposite occurs when the threat of new entrants is reduced, thereby reducing the possibility of new customer alternatives and allowing price increases or reduced marketing costs.

Step 5: How much substitute pressure will there be?

Substitute pressure arises when customers' needs can be met without your brand or one of its competitors. It can take many forms, from a medicine or technology with an entirely new mode of action to a new therapy protocol or even preventative lifestyle changes that effectively reduce the need for your product. Whatever the form of substitute, it diminishes the need for your product class and threatens profitability. Substitutes only occur under certain conditions and are disfavoured when those conditions don't exist. These opposing forces are shown in Figure 9.6.

In pharma and medtech, many costly products only help to manage, rather than resolve, the customers' problems. Equally, they often do so with significant side effects or inconvenience, and the heterogeneity of the market often includes segments with significant unmet needs. These factors create the conditions for substitutes, if substitutes are available. Increasing substitute pressure can shrink your product category, which might also increase direct rivalry (see Step 1), or it can create a new price comparator. A reduced threat of substitutes has the opposite effect, creating opportunities for growth in sales or profit.

SUBSTITUTE PRESSURE INCREASES WHEN:

The substitute would be profitable

The market is large and growing quickly

The substitute is proven to give better outcomes or results

Substitution is easy

Substitution would have large financial impact on customer

SUBSTITUTE PRESSURE DECREASES WHEN:

The substitute would be unprofitable

The market is small or declining

The substitute offers worse or unproven outcomes or results

Substitution is difficult

Substitution would have small financial impact on customer

Figure 9.6 *Market conditions that increase or decrease substitute pressure*

Step 6: What competitive threats and opportunities should we prioritise?

The final step in using the Competitive Pressure Analysis tool is to collate the work of the first five steps and prioritise the threats and opportunities from all forms of competition. The complexity of the factors means it's impossible to quantify each threat or opportunity with any accuracy. However, you can and should put the threats and opportunities you've identified into a relative order, based on the degree to which market conditions favour or disfavour each competitive pressure. Typically, this also implies a possible strategic response. Table 9.1 gives an example of this.

Table 9.1 *Example of the collation and prioritisation of competitive pressures*

PUTATIVE THREAT/ OPPORTUNITY	REASONS FOR THIS CHANGE	IMPLIED STRATEGIC RESPONSE
Strong increase in direct rivalry from branded me-too, based on price competition	Slowing of market growth means that growth targets of all current players can only be met by increasing market share	We will need to differentiate from me-too competitor, based either on product development or added-value services.
Strong increase in buyer pressure, based on demand for lower costs or better terms	Availability of me-too alternative and increasing involvement of payers in this high-budget-impact product category	As above, and we will need to take different account management approaches with customers of differing power.

PUTATIVE THREAT/ OPPORTUNITY	REASONS FOR THIS CHANGE	IMPLIED STRATEGIC RESPONSE
Moderate increase in supplier pressure, based on the difficulty and cost of maintaining a key account manager capability	Shortage of essential people with key account management skills	We will need to develop a programme to recruit and retain competent key account managers.
Significant decrease in new entrant pressure	Lack of easy entry point and slowing market growth	We need not prepare a counter strategy for new entrants, reducing the need to increase and refocus marketing resources.
Significant decrease in substitute pressure	Increasing evidence of lack of effectiveness and difficulty of lifestyle changes and counselling as substitute for our product category	We may be able to maintain pricing and reduce marketing costs in market segments previously under threat of substitution.

What should I do with my Competitive Pressure Analysis?

The outputs of your Competitive Pressure Analysis, which should look something like the right-hand column of Table 9.1, become one of the inputs into first the USUL and CLAL Reality Filters (Chapter 6) and then the SWOT Alignment (Chapter 5). The Competitive Pressure Analysis is an important contributor to the SWOT Alignment, which too often contains only product-related threats to sales; good SWOT Alignment needs to include threats to the brand's profitability from all directions.

Pragmatic advice for brand leaders

The main practical challenge in using the Competitive Pressure Analysis tool is the narrow, product-oriented view of competitors embedded in the culture of many pharma and medtech companies. Performing a proper analysis is a much broader, more thoughtful task than a narrow comparison of product features, which is what often passes for competitive analysis. Brand leaders will face objections that much of the analysis is already done elsewhere—buyer pressure in customer analysis, for example. This is partly true, as the information may be gathered already; but it is the job of the brand leader to make sure that information from any source is used to identify all competitive pressures. You may also face the objection that the information is beyond the brand team's scope. For example, possible acquisition targets that allow new entrants are generally considered by the business development team, not marketing. In this case, you must lead the brand team to cooperate with those in the organisation who hold the relevant information. In any case, the brand team must appreciate that it's their job to understand every pressure on their brand's profitability and, consequently, that any brand strategy not built on that knowledge is weak.

Strong brand strategies understand the customer: Using Contextual Segmentation to identify opportunities and threats from customer differences

Strong brand strategies understand and use the differences and similarities between your customers. This chapter guides your understanding of how professionals, payers and patients combine to segment your market and the opportunities and threats that arise from this.

When should I use Contextual Segmentation?

Segmentation is so fundamental to brand strategy that it immediately follows market definition (Chapter 2). This means you need to use the Contextual Segmentation tool in all but the simplest markets, where traditional segmentation is sufficient. The inputs to Contextual Segmentation are the motivating needs you identified when defining the market. The outputs are twofold: first, a well understood and defined set of market segments that are used in the Focus Matrix (Chapter 7); second, a list of opportunities and threats that arise from these segments, which feed into the SWOT Alignment (Chapter 5) via the Reality Filters (Chapter 6). Whilst all the tools described in this book are important, Contextual Segmentation is arguably the most important. Theodore Levitt was right when he said, 'If you're not thinking segmentation, you're not thinking'. Where Contextual Segmentation fits into the brand strategy process is shown in Figure 10.1.

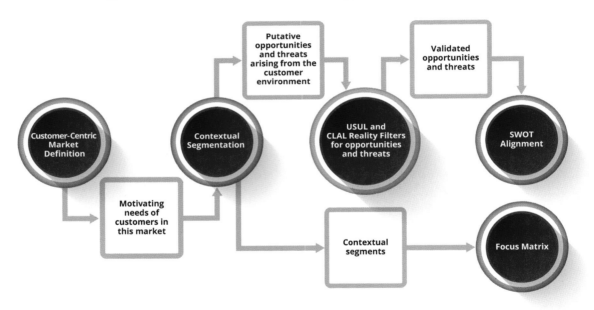

Figure 10.1 *Where Contextual Segmentation fits into the brand strategy process*

Why is Contextual Segmentation especially important in pharma and medtech markets?

In the past, pharma and medtech markets shared two characteristics—healthcare professionals decided which brand to use, and the shared backgrounds and organisations of these professionals meant that their motivating needs were similar. Recently, however, fundamental shifts in our market have transformed these characteristics.

Firstly, the healthcare professional is now only part of the decision. Payers play a role that is dominant for some products and influential in many. At the same time, patients have also become part of the purchasing decision, either because their clinical needs are stratified or because (enabled by Google) they are no longer deferent to medical authority. The degree of involvement of each of these three stakeholders in brand selection varies greatly between product categories but it's now no longer true to say that the healthcare professional is the customer.

Secondly, the motivating needs of these three decision makers are more complex and varied than ever. Professionals differ in, for example, their technical interests and their engagement with the patient. Payers vary in their strategies to control costs and their attitude to professionals' preferences. Patients vary in their clinical, aesthetic, financial and emotional needs. These various motivations differ greatly between markets but we can no longer give a single answer to the question, 'What does our customer want?'

These two fundamental changes combine to make pharma and medtech markets more heterogeneous, along more dimensions than in earlier times when brand choices were made by similarly minded professionals alone. Traditional segmentation, which worked in that simpler world, no longer works today. This is why Contextual Segmentation is especially important in pharma and medtech markets.

What is Contextual Segmentation and how does it work?

Traditional segmentation groups together customers who have the same motivating needs (see Chapter 2) but works well only if there's a single decision maker. Contextual Segmentation is an evolutionary adaptation to markets where professionals, payers and patients are all involved in the choice of brand. It works by identifying variations within each of the three groups and combining those differences to determine the most important brand choice contexts. It is the decision context that is segmented, not the customers, and each of these contextual segments implies opportunities and threats of some kind. Contextual Segmentation is much more sophisticated but more effective than traditional segmentation and requires some skill to perform. Those companies that have mastered it do so in five steps.

Exercise 10.1

Using the Customer-Centric Market Definition you developed in Chapter 2, identify the most important motivating need of patients in your market. Estimate the distribution of that need (Figure 10.2). Strong answers will identify the need that most powerfully motivates and differentiates patients' brand preference. Weak answers will use motivating needs that do not differentiate well because most patients are similar on this dimension, or motivating needs that do not strongly drive brand preference.

Step 1: What needs differentiate our patients?

Although all patients in your customer-centrically defined market share the same hygiene needs, their motivating needs differ in many ways (Chapter 2). Typical differences might be clinical or technological: disease stage, patient phenotype or comorbidities, for example. Or they might be non-clinical, such as financial, aesthetic or attitudinal differences. Whatever they are, these differences drive brand preference and, when the patient influences the brand choice, they contribute to market segmentation. Mapping these differences begins with selecting the motivating need that most powerfully drives brand preference and estimating its distribution across the patient population. An illustration is shown in Figure 10.2.

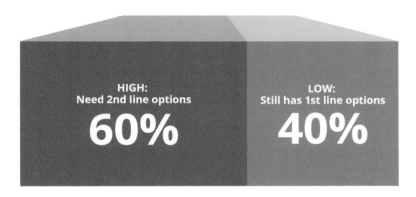

HIGH:
Need 2nd line options
60%

LOW:
Still has 1st line options
40%

Patients' clinical need for treatment options
(e.g. 1st, 2nd line)

Figure 10.2 *Example of the distribution of patients' motivating needs*

Even without considering professionals and payers, patients with different motivating needs will have different preferences for any given brand offer, so they are an important component of Contextual Segmentation.

Step 2: What needs differentiate our professionals?

Although all professionals in your customer-centrically defined market share the same hygiene needs, their motivating needs differ in many ways (Chapter 2). Typical differences might be clinical or technological: preference for mode of action, concern with ease of use or time to result, for example. Or they might be non-clinical, such as risk tolerance or need for professional status, for example. Whatever they are, these differences drive brand preference and, to the extent that the professional is allowed to choose between brands, they contribute to market segmentation. Mapping these differences begins with selecting the motivating need that most powerfully drives brand preference and estimating its distribution across all professionals in the market. An illustration is shown in Figure 10.3.

Even without considering patients and payers, professionals with differing motivating needs will have different preferences for any given brand offer, so they are an important component of Contextual Segmentation.

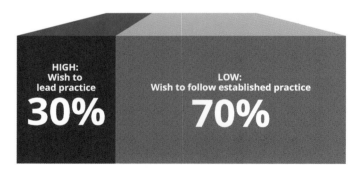

HIGH:
Wish to
lead practice
30%

LOW:
Wish to follow established practice
70%

Professionals' need to be innovative

Figure 10.3 *Example of the distribution of professionals' motivating needs*

Step 3: What needs differentiate our payers?

Although all payers in your market are focused on economic efficiency, they approach it in different ways. Typical differences might include financial priorities, such as reducing costs vs increasing efficiency, or they might reflect their attitudes to value, such as cost-focus vs outcome-focus. Such differences between payers drive their brand preferences. As with patients and professionals, mapping these differences involves identifying the motivating need that most powerfully drives brand preference and differentiates between payers. An example of this is shown in Figure 10.4.

Exercise 10.3

Using the Customer-Centric Market Definition you developed in Chapter 2, identify the most important motivating need of payers in your market. Estimate the distribution of that need, as in Figure 10.4. Strong answers will identify the need that most powerfully motivates and differentiates payers' brand preference. Weak answers will use motivating needs that do not differentiate well because most payers are similar on this dimension, or motivating needs that do not strongly drive brand preference.

HIGH:
Value oriented
40%

LOW:
Price oriented
60%

Payers' need for health economic understanding

Figure 10.4 *Example of the distribution of payers' motivating needs*

As with professionals and patients, payers with different motivating needs will have different preferences for any given brand offer, so they are an important component of Contextual Segmentation.

Step 4: What contextual segments are important in our market?

The fourth step in using the Contextual Segmentation tool is to combine the patient, professional and payer motivations to create a three-dimensional contextual segmentation map. See the example in Figure 10.5.

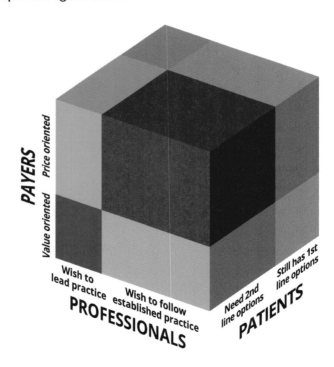

Figure 10.5 *Example three-dimensional contextual segmentation map*

This example is based on those in the preceding three steps in which, for the decision maker, only one motivating need with a simple, bifurcated distribution was considered. In practice, it's possible to consider two or even three motivating needs for each decision maker involved, and for these to have more complex distributions. Although this leads to a much more segmented market, the principle is exactly as shown in this simpler example.

The important point is that every box shown in this three-dimensional map is a different combination of patient, professional and payer motivating needs: a different contextual segment. Each brand choice decision made within a contextual segment will be driven by similar preferences and will usually result in the same choice. Equally, brand choice decisions made in different contextual segments will be driven by different preferences and will usually result in a different choice.

Exercise 10.4

Combine your patients', professionals' and payers' motivating needs from the earlier exercises to construct a three-dimensional contextual segmentation map for your market, using Figure 10.5 as a guide. Strong answers will identify at least eight contextual segments in which brand choice decisions are driven by motivations that are shared within the segment but distinct from other segments. Weak answers will either include needs that don't drive behaviour or will neglect needs that do.

Step 5: What opportunities and threats arise from these segments?

The final step in using the Contextual Segmentation tool is to identify the threats and opportunities that arise from your contextual segments. Generally, there are four pairs of threats and opportunities that can possibly arise from a segment, shown in Table 10.1.

Table 10.1 *Generalised threats and opportunities that emerge from Contextual Segmentation*

A CONTEXTUAL SEGMENT REPRESENTS AN OPPORTUNITY WHEN...	A CONTEXTUAL SEGMENT REPRESENTS A THREAT WHEN...
... it's some combination of large, profitable and growing, presenting an opportunity for growth.	... it's some combination of small, unprofitable and declining, threatening decline of current business.
... we either do or can easily meet its needs, presenting an opportunity to win share at good ROI.	...we neither do nor can easily meet its needs, threatening to consume resources at low ROI.
... it currently consumes significant resources at low ROI, presenting the opportunity to divert resources to a higher ROI segment.	... it's demanding of valuable resources, threatening to divert resources at low ROI.
... it positively influences other segments, presenting an opportunity for positive synergy between segments.	... it negatively influences other segments, threatening negative synergy between segments.

Exercise 10.5

Using the output of Exercise 10.4, and Tables 10.1 and 10.2 as a guide, create a list of opportunities and threats that arise from your market's contextual segmentation. Strong answers will identify a specific opportunity or threat from each contextual segment. Weak answers will identify a large number of non-specific threats and opportunities.

Step 5 involves using Table 10.1 and the contextual segments from Step 4 to identify the specific opportunities and threats presented by the Contextual Segmentation of your market (see the example in Table 10.2).

Table 10.2 *Examples of specific threats and opportunities that emerge from Contextual Segmentation*

CONTEXTUAL SEGMENT CHARACTERISTICS	THIS CONTEXTUAL SEGMENT REPRESENTS AN OPPORTUNITY TO...	THIS CONTEXTUAL SEGMENT REPRESENTS A THREAT IF...
The segment offers low returns and we already meet its needs well.	... carefully and selectively reduce resources, whilst maintaining share, and direct them to other segments.	... we allocate more resources than are needed.
The segment offers high returns and we don't yet but can easily meet its needs well.	... focus sales and marketing resources to generate growth at good ROI in the short term.	... we under-resource this segment.
The segment offers high returns but we don't yet meet its needs, and to do so will take significant effort.	... allocate resources towards developing value propositions in order to generate growth at good ROI in the medium term.	... we waste sales and marketing resources on this segment before we've developed a strong value proposition for it.
The segment offers low returns, we don't yet meet its needs, and to do so will take significant effort.	... divert all resources from this segment and take business here only as and when it arises and can be won with little effort.	... we allow this segment to divert significant resources from other segments.

What should I do with my Contextual Segmentation?

There are two uses for the Contextual Segmentation tool's outputs. First, you should now have a manageable number of opportunities and threats that arise from the heterogeneity of your customers' needs. Together with the outputs of other tools, these can now be fed into the USUL and CLAL Reality Filters (Chapter 6) and, once validated, into the SWOT Alignment (Chapter 5). Second, these contextual segments, as well as presenting opportunities and threats, also vary in how attractive they are and how difficult they are to win. These segments are the inputs for the Focus Matrix (Chapter 7).

Pragmatic advice for brand leaders

Contextual Segmentation is a significant change from traditional segmentation, which means that you should expect significant resistance to its use. In practice, this resistance comes in two main forms. The first is that your organisation doesn't have the information about patient, professional and payer motivations to do Contextual Segmentation. Unless you're new to the market, this is probably untrue (although it may seem true if you lack quantitative data about motivating needs, which is often the case). But even lacking quantitative research, we often have a lot of soft knowledge about motivations, which can be inferred from current usage and sale teams' implicit knowledge. Also, key knowledge gaps can be filled using the Hypothesis Loop (Chapter 13). It's the task of the brand leader to overcome this over-reliance on one form of information. The second objection is that the heterogeneity uncovered by Contextual Segmentation cannot be addressed when product development takes many years. This is a misunderstanding that arises from a product-oriented culture. Contextual segments have similar needs in terms of the core product (the molecule or technology). Their differing characteristic needs rarely imply new products. Instead, their needs can usually be met by changes to the Concentric Value Proposition, such as service, or minor product-line extensions (see Chapter 14). It's the job of the brand leader to make clear that the offer is not the same thing as the product.

Strong brand strategies compete in the future: Using Emergent Properties Analysis to identify future opportunities and threats

Strong brand strategies understand and use the wider market drivers shaping your market. This chapter shows you how to identify those factors and how they combine to create opportunities and threats.

When should I use Emergent Properties Analysis?

The Emergent Properties Analysis tool provides insight into how your market will change in the future, so it can't be used until you have defined your market from the customers' perspective (Chapter 2). It should then be used early in the brand planning process and is especially useful if your market is changing in important ways. The inputs of Emergent

Properties Analysis are facts about how the wider market environment is changing, rather than the immediate context of customers and competitors. Its outputs are the opportunities and threats arising from that wider context. After being validated by the Reality Filters (Chapter 6), these outputs become the inputs into the SWOT Alignment (Chapter 5). Where Emergent Properties Analysis fits into the brand strategy process is shown in Figure 11.1.

Figure 11.1 *Where Emergent Properties Analysis fits into the brand strategy process*

Why is Emergent Properties Analysis especially important in pharma and medtech markets?

The need for Emergent Properties Analysis comes from the fact that the life sciences market is a complex, adaptive system, comparable to the weather system or a biological system like the rainforest. This fact has two important, practical implications.

The first is that, just like the weather, pharma and medtech markets can't be forecast except in a very localised, short-term way. If we want to anticipate their long-term direction, we must use ideas from complexity and evolutionary science and look for emergent properties, these being characteristics of the market that result from the interaction of its many different parts.

The second is that, like all complex systems, pharma and medtech markets don't change steadily. They evolve in bursts of change that punctuate longer periods of relative stability. The last decades of the 20th and first years of the 21st century were one such period of slow change but, in recent years, our market has entered a period of rapid change. Given how difficult it is for industries like ours to adapt to change, this makes it important to anticipate its future.

So, pharma and medtech's burst of rapid change is making it essential to anticipate the future, whilst the complexity of our market makes traditional predictive forecasting less useful. This is why Emergent Properties Analysis is especially important to our industry.

What is Emergent Properties Analysis and how does it work?

Emergent Properties Analysis is a tool for understanding how your market's social and technological environments create opportunities and threats to which your brand strategy must adapt. It begins by widely scanning your market environment to identify the factors that shape your market. It then looks for the complex interactions between those factors. Finally, it draws out the market changes caused by those interactions and to which your brand strategy must adapt. Emergent Properties Analysis is a systematic, skilled process and those firms that have mastered it do so in four steps.

Exercise 11.1

Using Figure 11.2 as a guide, identify the most important factors in your market environment. Strong answers will identify 20 or more factors distributed across all four boxes of the grid. Weak answers will identify a small number of factors or will omit parts of the environment.

Step 1: What are our social and technological environments?

The first step of Emergent Properties Analysis requires you to look broadly for factors that might influence your market but that are often missed by traditional, product-oriented situation analyses. An effective approach to this is the environmental factor grid shown in Figure 11.2. Applying this to the context of your market identifies the most important factors that make up your market environment.

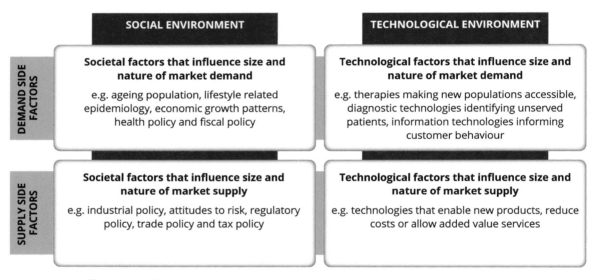

Figure 11.2 *A framework for scanning your market's wider environment*

Step 2: How is our environment changing?

The second step in Emergent Properties Analysis is to identify how the factors identified in Step 1 are changing, since it is change in the environment that will shape changes in your market. An effective approach to this is to identify both changes and their immediate, first-order implications for your market. This is illustrated in the example shown in Table 11.1.

Table 11.1 *Example of market changes and their first-order implications*

Market factor	Changes observed/anticipated	First-order implication
1. Population demographics	Significant increase in middle-aged and elderly population	Increased prevalence of our targeted disease and therefore market potential
2. Lifestyle trends	Increased prevalence of good lifestyle choices	Postponement of disease development to later life with more comorbidities
3. Economic growth	Sustained slow economic growth	Reduced government revenues
4. Personal wealth distribution	Increased polarisation of personal income and wealth	Polarisation of discretionary spend across population
5. Health policy	Focusing of health policy on managing increase in chronic demand	Reduction in payer interest in improved outcomes or other secondary benefits
6. Fiscal policy	Growing reluctance to increase government spending and limitation to further reallocation	Reduced real terms spending on health relative to demand
7. Attitude to risk	Increasing social and political sensitivity to clinical risk	Greater business risk from adverse events and political pressure for increased regulation
8. Regulatory policy	Increasing demand for real-world data and gradual approvals	Increasing costs and difficulty of achieving regulatory approval

135

Market factor	Changes observed/anticipated	First-order implication
9. Market access policy	Increasing pressure for generic substitution and health economic justification for non-generics	Increased costs and difficulty of achieving market access
10. Healthcare provision	Increasing focus on cost control via contracting and partnerships	Emergence of contract purchasers and provision by contractors
11. Trade policy	Shrinking nontariff barriers to foreign provision of goods and services	Likely entry of low cost competitors
12. Diagnostic technology	New technologies enabling low cost point-of-care screening	Increased volume of early stage patients
13. Therapeutic technology	New technologies enabling treatment of previously untreatable patients	Increased volume of severe patients
14. Information technology	Patient monitoring technology enabling payers to monitor cost effectiveness of treatment approaches	Increased pressure for and potential to provide cost effectiveness information
15. Therapeutic technology	Improved diagnostic technology allowing better patient stratification	Increased potential to target and manage patients individually
16. Manufacturing technology	New manufacturing and logistics technology allowing lower manufacturing costs of core molecule	Reduced costs of generics
17. Mobile technology	Access to mobile technology becoming ubiquitous	Possibility to use mobile technology to access patients more directly
18. Social attitudes	Reducing patient deference to medical professionals	Emergence of self-management patient segment

The key to completing this step is to look widely across the environment for changes that influence your market, often in indirect ways.

Step 3: What are the interactions in our environment?

The third step in Emerging Properties Analysis recognises that the first-order implications identified in Step 2 shape the market not by themselves but only in combination with each other. It's the interaction of these first-order implications that is important to the brand. So, Step 3 involves identifying how the first-order implications combine to create second-order implications. This is a process of thoughtful judgement that cannot be reduced to a mechanical process. An example is given in Table 11.2.

Exercise 11.2

Using the results of Exercise 11.1, and using Table 11.1 as a guide, create your own list of market environment changes and their first-order implications. A strong answer will usually identify changes in most environmental factors and first-order implications for each of the changing factors. A weak answer will fail to look widely, fail to identify changes in the environment or overlook their implications for the brand.

Table 11.2 *Example of second-order implications of changes in the market environment*

FIRST-ORDER IMPLICATIONS (FROM TABLE 11.1)
1. Increased prevalence of our targeted disease and therefore market potential
2. Postponement of disease development to later life with more comorbidities
3. Reduced government revenues
4. Polarisation of discretionary spend across population
5. Reduction in payer interest in improved outcomes or other secondary benefits
6. Reduced real terms spending on health relative to demand
7. Greater business risk from adverse events and political pressure for increased regulation
8. Increasing costs and difficulty of achieving regulatory approval
9. Increased costs and difficulty of achieving market access
10. Emergence of contract purchasers and provision by contractors
11. Likely entry of low cost competitors
12. Increased volume of early stage patients
13. Increased volume of severe patients
14. Increased pressure for and potential to provide cost effectiveness information
15. Increased potential to target and manage patients individually
16. Reduced costs of generics
17. Possibility to use mobile technology to access patients more directly
18. Emergence of self-management patient segment

SECOND-ORDER IMPLICATIONS	
1+3+5+6+12+13	The demands to treat our disease area will exceed the funds available to meet that demand, resulting in lower per capita spend that, combined with the high fixed costs of providers, will focus cost control attention onto the cost of our products.
2+4+5+10+15+17	This disease area will become an obvious candidate for outsourcing to a contracted provider, resulting in a shift in who we are dealing with and their motivating needs.
5+9+11+16	Pressure will grow to treat most patients with generics that will increasingly be much cheaper than branded products, making market access much more difficult.
5+7+8+9	It will become increasingly difficult to create product modifications that provide value, compared to generics, in the eyes of the payer.
4+5+17+18	There will emerge a gap between what traditional providers will make available and what is technologically and financially accessible to an educated and affluent patient segment.

Step 4: What are the opportunities and threats created by those interactions?

The final step in Emerging Properties Analysis is to understand the second-order implications in terms of the threats and opportunities they create. Again, this is a matter of judgement, but if Steps 1 to 3 have been carried out with care, the process will be relatively straightforward. Implications that are positive, such as those that increase market size or play to an organisational strength, are opportunities. Those that are negative, such as those that decrease market size or exacerbate an organisational weakness, are threats. This is illustrated in Table 11.3.

Table 11.3 *Example of the opportunities and threats emerging from the market environment*

SECOND-ORDER IMPLICATIONS (FROM TABLE 11.2)	OPPORTUNITIES AND THREATS
The demands to treat our disease area will exceed the funds available to meet that demand, resulting in lower per capita spend that, combined with the high fixed costs of providers, will focus cost control attention onto the cost of our products.	There is a threat of increasing cost controls on our products either directly or indirectly.
This disease area will become an obvious candidate for outsourcing to a contracted provider, resulting in a shift in who we are dealing with and their motivating needs.	There is an opportunity for us to develop into a contracted provider. There is a threat that our interaction with providers will be intermediated by large-scale, consolidated specialist providers.
Pressure will grow to treat most patients with generics that will increasingly be much cheaper than branded products, making market access much more difficult.	There is a threat that branded products will be restricted to a very small volume part of the overall market.
It will become increasingly difficult to create product modifications that provide value, compared to generics, in the eyes of the payer.	There is a threat that we could waste resources on developing line extension value propositions that are not attractive to any segment of the market.
There will emerge a gap between what traditional providers will make available and what is technologically and financially accessible to an educated and affluent patient segment.	There is an opportunity to address a high-margin segment of affluent, self-managing patients directly.

The key is to think more broadly than the current strategy and envisage what might be possible. When Step 4 is complete, the result will be a number of threats and opportunities (typically five to ten) that arise from changes in your brand's social and technological environments.

What should I do with my Emergent Properties Analysis?

When you've completed the Emergent Properties Analysis, you will have identified around five to ten opportunities and threats that arise from changes in your market's social and technological environment. These outputs, along with opportunities and threats identified through other tools, become the inputs to your SWOT Alignment (Chapter 5) via validation using the Reality Filters (Chapter 6). As with the other tools, the value of Emergent Property Analysis

Exercise 11.3

Using the first-order implications from Exercise 11.2 and following the example in Table 11.2, consider how your first-order implications interact to create second-order implications. Strong answers will identify sufficient interaction so that the number of second-order implications is between half and a quarter of the number of first-order implications. Weak answers will fail to consider enough interactions and will identify many fewer or many more than this number.

Exercise 11.4

Using the outputs of Exercise 11.3, and Table 11.3 as a guide, identify the opportunities and threats specific to your brand that emerge from changes to the social and technological environments. A strong answer will identify five to ten clear outputs, balanced between opportunities and threats. A weak answer will identify many more or less than this, or will show an imbalance between opportunities and threats.

141

lies not only in its outputs but also in the shared view the brand team will develop as it works through the process.

Pragmatic advice for brand leaders

As with many of the other tools in this book, Emergent Properties Analysis replaces a familiar, simple but ineffective process (the SLEPT or PEST analysis) with one that demands significantly more effort in return for a much more useful output. It would be naïve not to expect resistance to this change. Resistance usually comes in two forms. The first is silo thinking, which asserts that many of the technological and social factors lie outside the scope of the brand team's work, either at corporate level or in another function, such as R&D. This is dangerously blinkered thinking. Whilst some factors may be considered in other parts of the company, it's the brand team's job to think broadly and deeply about anything that influences the success of their brand. The brand leader has to embed this thinking in the team. The second form of resistance concerns timescale. Brand teams can, with some justification, claim that the opportunities and threats arising from the social and technological environments won't affect the brand for years, long after their planning cycle. This is selfishly short-term thinking. It's the team's job to act in the brand's long-term interests. Again, it is the job of the brand leader to make sure the team absorb this truth.

Strong brand strategies anticipate the market: Using the Product Category Life Cycle to predict customer and competitor behaviour

Strong brand strategies understand and allow for what customers and competitors will do next. This chapter helps you to understand how adoption and imitation shape your market over time and how to anticipate those changes.

When should I use the Product Category Life Cycle?

The Product Category Life Cycle tool (PCLC) can be used at any time in the brand strategy process after you've created a Customer-Centric Market Definition (Chapter 2) and before using the Reality Filters (Chapter 6). But it's most useful when used after other tools, such as Competitive Pressure Analysis (Chapter 9), Contextual

Segmentation (Chapter 10) and Emergent Properties Analysis (Chapter 11), because the understanding gained from these tools improves the application and outcomes of PCLC. PCLC's outcomes are anticipated opportunities and threats that become inputs into the SWOT Alignment (Chapter 5) after validation by the Reality Filters (Chapter 6). The place of the PCLC in the brand strategy process is shown in Figure 12.1.

Figure 12.1 *Where the Product Category Life Cycle fits into the brand strategy process*

Why is the Product Category Life Cycle tool especially important in pharma and medtech markets?

All markets are shaped by the interaction of two things: how suppliers innovate and imitate, and how customers adopt those innovations and imitations. All brand strategies must understand this dynamic but, in pharma and medtech, two peculiarities of the market make it especially important.

The first is that, compared to other markets, both supplier innovation and customer adoption is unusual. As in all markets, some suppliers lead innovation and others follow, but pharma and medtech's technological and social complexities are unusual. Issues such as regulatory approval, loss of exclusivity, and genericisation all influence innovation and imitation. And factors such as opinion leaders, market access, and politics all influence adoption and uptake. This makes anticipating the future market more difficult, but it also makes product development a longer process which, in turn, makes anticipating the market more necessary.

The second peculiarity of the life sciences market is the way in which it has corrupted the product life cycle idea. In academic research and other industries, the product life cycle concept is used to explain changes in the overall market, which includes all products of a given type. For example, we think of the life cycles of vinyl, cassettes, CDs, downloads and streaming to explain changes in the recorded music industry. But the product-oriented culture of pharma and medtech has limited the concept to individual products within a category. For example, we talk about product life cycle management, meaning the tactics to respond to imitation of our brand. This corruption of the life cycle concept is of limited use in anticipating and understanding the future of the market.

So, the need to anticipate a complex market and the corruption of the tool for doing so is what makes the Product Category Life Cycle tool especially important in pharma and medtech.

What is the Product Category Life Cycle and how does it work?

The Product Category Life Cycle is a tool for extrapolating from the past and present to predict the future of your market. It's based on the generalisation that certain characteristics of the market change over time in a way that's predictable enough to be useful. The inputs into the PCLC are observations about the current market that are readily apparent, such as the number, type and share of competing products. These are aggregated to enable a judgement about the product category's current life cycle stage. This in turn allows predictions about what will happen next, and these predictions, in the form of anticipated opportunities and threats, are the outputs of the tool. Like almost all strategic management tools, using PCLC is craft rather than science and those firms that have mastered it do so in four steps.

> **Exercise 12.1**
>
> Using the idea of customer-perceived interchangeability, list all the products that make up your brand's product category and give that category a descriptive label. Good answers will include all products that the customer could use to address his or her basic needs with little change in practice. Weak answers will either include products that are significantly different substitutes or will exclude products that differ only in minor ways.

Step 1: What product category are we in?

The first step when using the PCLC is to define the product category correctly. A definition that's too wide (e.g. 'in vitro diagnostics' or 'cardiovascular drugs') or too narrow (e.g., 'branded, premium-priced, proton-pump inhibitors' or 'premium hydrocolloid dressings for decubitus ulcers') produces meaningless outputs. The correct balance is achieved through a customer-centric perspective. Your brand's product category includes all products that the customer perceives he or she could use interchangeably to address the same basic need. Examples of typical categories are 'clinical chemistry analysers', 'ACE inhibitors' and 'negative pressure wound therapy'.

Step 2: What are our indicators of life cycle stage?

Just as hair colour, skin texture and body shape are indicators of a human's life cycle stage, certain market factors indicate the PCLC stage; and the second step when using the PCLC is to identify the most useful market factors. The predictive value of different factors varies between markets, and part of the craft of the PCLC is to choose those factors that are the most useful indicators in practice. The most useful vary predictably over time and are easy to observe. Examples of these are given in Table 12.1.

Table 12.1 *Examples of Product Category Life Cycle factors*

PCLC FACTOR
Number and size of competitors supplying product category
Rate of product category growth
Variety of technologies in the product category
Degree and basis of differentiation between competitors in the product category
Pricing behaviour within the product category
Market share distribution within the category
Marketing objectives of firms within the product category
Patterns of marketing communications activity within the product category

Step 3: What do those indicators tell us?

The third step when using the PCLC is to infer the life cycle stage from the chosen indicators. Table 12.2 shows the normal relationship between the PCLC stage and market factors. Importantly, at any one time, different factors may indicate different stages; applying the

Exercise 12.2

Using Table 12.1 as a guide, identify the factors that are most useful for characterising your brand's PCLC stage. Good answers will identify several factors that are both observable and change significantly over time. Weak answers will identify only a few factors that are hard to observe and/or vary little over time.

PCLC involves making a balanced judgement across all factors. When most factors indicate one stage, this is straightforward. When the factors are divided across two adjacent stages, this implies a transition between the two stages. If the factors suggest a spread of results, this is usually a sign of either poor category definition (Step 1) or inaccurate data gathering.

Table 12.2 *Examples of the correlation between life cycle markers and life cycle stage*

PCLC FACTOR	EMBRYONIC	GROWTH	MATURITY	DECLINE
Number and size of competitors supplying product category	Very few, typically only one or two firms of small size	Many new competitors enter, mostly small; some larger firms emerge as stage progresses	Some competitors exit or reduce their activity significantly, leaving a small number of players dominating the market	Most competitors exit, leaving only two to four significant competitors
Rate of product category growth	Growth is erratic and slow as the new product category attempts to replace the preceding one	Growth is fast and less erratic as new product category is accepted, but begins to slow towards end of stage	Growth is slow or non-existent relative to overall market growth, turning negative at end of the stage	Growth is negative as category shrinks and is replaced by new category

PCLC FACTOR	EMBRYONIC	GROWTH	MATURITY	DECLINE
Variety of technologies in the product category	Competing products have significantly different technologies or designs	Designs and technologies converge on one type as standards emerge	Dominant products in the market share very similar design or technology	Differences in product design become negligible
Degree and basis of differentiation between competitors in the product category	Competitors are strongly differentiated on basis of design or technology	Design and technology differentiation decreases and competition shifts to performance factors	Performance differentiation declines and competition shifts to non-product factors, such as branding and service	Competitors become almost identical and competition shifts to price alone
Pricing behaviour within the product category	Highly variable as competitors try to find acceptable price point	Becoming less variable and converging into two or more price levels	Polarisation into premium and economy competitor groups	Reduction in prices as market commoditises
Market share distribution within the product category	New category has little share of market, which is evenly split between few competitors	Market share fluctuates then begins to aggregate around a few dominant competitors	Market consolidates, with most of the market held by a small number of competitors	Market consolidates into duopoly or oligopoly

PCLC FACTOR	EMBRYONIC	GROWTH	MATURITY	DECLINE
Marketing objectives of firms within the product category	To convert usage from preceding product category	To convert usage from preceding category and to win share within category	To maximise market share profitably within category	To defend against replacement category and to maintain profit as prices decline
Patterns of marketing communications activity within the product category	Aimed at gaining endorsement for new category from opinion leaders	Aimed at making new category de-facto standard and building brand	Aimed at optimising share and price within category	Marketing communications activity declines but is aimed at defending profitability

Step 4: What opportunities and threats can we anticipate?

Exercise 12.4

Using your judgement of the PCLC stage from Exercise 12.3, and Table 12.3 as a guide, anticipate how the marker characteristics will change in your brand's product category, and the implications for your brand. Strong answers will identify several opportunities and threats and form a judgement on their importance and timescale. Weak answers will fail to identify the implications of the PCLC maturation.

The final step when using the PCLC is to anticipate the opportunities and threats that will arise as your brand's PCLC matures. This involves the fundamental assumption that the indicator factors will progress as indicated in Table 12.2. Not all indicators will change at the same rate, so change can't be anticipated with certainty; but generally, as the market matures, each of the indicator characteristics will change as described in Table 12.2.

This predictable change allows you to anticipate opportunities and threats both in the short and long term. For example, if your brand's PCLC stage appears to be late growth, you can anticipate that the rate of market growth might decline as your PCLC moves into maturity. If your category is embryonic, the number of competitors might increase as you go from the embryonic to the growth stage. As a general guideline, competitive intensity increases over the course of the PCLC. An example of this anticipation is shown in Table 12.3.

Table 12.3 *Anticipating the opportunities and threats from the Product Category Life Cycle*

AT EMBRYONIC STAGE	AT GROWTH STAGE	AT MATURITY STAGE	AT DECLINE STAGE
Opportunity to win share from preceding product category	Opportunity to establish your design/technology as the standard	Opportunity to build strong brand	Opportunity to optimise pricing as competitors exit market
Opportunity to win support of opinion leaders	Opportunity to compete on performance differences	Opportunity to create non-product differentiation	Opportunities to compete with adaptive pricing strategies
Threat of new competitors with similar technologies	Threat from standardisation onto other technologies	Threat from consolidation of competitors into larger, stronger competitors	Threat of low cost competitors
Threat of wasting resources on 'laggard' customers	Threat from emergence of lower cost competitors	Threat from comparison to low cost competitors	Threat from newly emerging replacement-product category

What should I do with my Product Category Life Cycle predictions?

The PCLC tool results in a set of perceived opportunities and threats that arise as supplier innovation and imitation and customer adoption work together to create market maturity. These become the inputs into SWOT Alignment (Chapter 5), after validation by the Reality Filters (Chapter 6). In addition, the discussion necessary to complete the PCLC also helps to develop a shared understanding within the brand team.

Pragmatic advice for brand leaders

As with some of the other tools in this book, such as Contextual Segmentation and Competitive Pressure Analysis, the PCLC tool is quite different from current practice (which has a similar name in most pharma and medtech markets). This means that it will meet with indirect resistance as brand team members perceive the benefits to be limited. In fact, the PCLC is a wider, deeper and much more useful tool than traditional approaches to product life cycle management, which are really shorthand for tactical line-extension activity. A second issue with the PCLC is its qualitative nature. Although many factors, such as market growth and numbers of competitors, can be quantified, the judgement of the PCLC is inevitably qualitative and imprecise. In the scientific cultures dominant in pharma and medtech, this is often used to devalue the method. In actual fact, a judgement founded on multiple qualitative inputs is more valuable than a simplistic implication based on a single hard number. Overcoming the 'we do that already' and 'it's too qualitative' objections are both important tasks for the brand leader.

CHAPTER 13

Strong brand strategies are built on insight: Using the Hypothesis Loop to see what your competitors don't

Strong brand strategies are based on valuable and unique insight that your competitors don't possess. This chapter explains what true market insight is and how it can be created from the information that you already have.

When should I use the Hypothesis Loop?

If you already know the market well and the other tools have provided a good understanding of the critical success factors (Chapter 5), you may not need to use the Hypothesis Loop. It becomes valuable when you find weaknesses in your market knowledge—for example, when you're not clear on how to achieve your brand objectives, or when previous brand strategies haven't given you the results you expected. The inputs into the Hypothesis Loop are existing market knowledge about customer and competitor behaviour. The output is some genuine market insight that will help guide your brand strategy. The place of the Hypothesis Loop in the brand strategy process is shown in Figure 13.1.

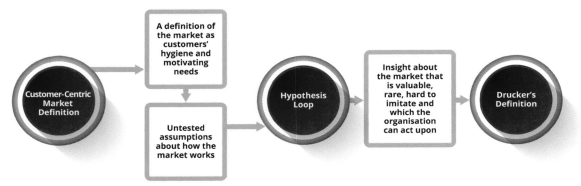

Figure 13.1 *Where the Hypothesis Loop fits into the brand strategy process*

Why is the Hypothesis Loop especially important in pharma and medtech markets?

The need for the Hypothesis Loop in pharma and medtech markets is driven by two obvious characteristics of the market. The first is that our industry is rich in data and becoming more so. Paradoxically, this creates a problem, as ever-larger data 'haystacks' make it harder to find the 'needles' of insight on which we can build brand strategy. As Figure 13.2 shows, the terms data, information, knowledge and insight, although often used interchangeably, have distinct meanings. True market insight is knowledge that is a valuable organisational strength (see Chapter 6). However, as the data, information and knowledge available to us increases constantly, brand teams spend more time shuffling it all around without actually creating true market insight.

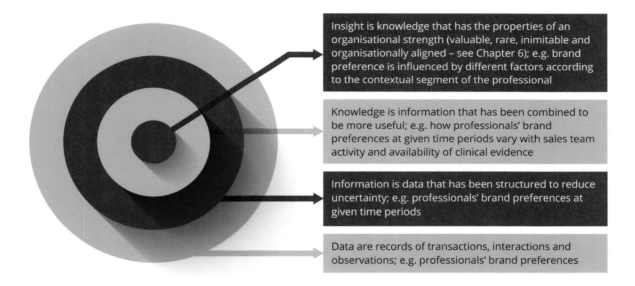

Insight is knowledge that has the properties of an organisational strength (valuable, rare, inimitable and organisationally aligned – see Chapter 6); e.g. brand preference is influenced by different factors according to the contextual segment of the professional

Knowledge is information that has been combined to be more useful; e.g. how professionals' brand preferences at given time periods vary with sales team activity and availability of clinical evidence

Information is data that has been structured to reduce uncertainty; e.g. professionals' brand preferences at given time periods

Data are records of transactions, interactions and observations; e.g. professionals' brand preferences

Figure 13.2 *Differences between data, information, knowledge and insight*

The second characteristic is that our industry is rapidly and fundamentally changing. This has the important, often overlooked, implication of very quickly making old knowledge less useful. For example, insights into professionals' preferences, gathered when professionals alone made choices, are less useful in an age when payers and patients also influence the decision. The decaying value of existing insights means that the ability to create new ones is valuable to the brand team.

So, the erosion of existing insights and the difficulty of finding new ones in a haystack of data make the Hypothesis Loop tool especially important in pharma and medtech.

What is the Hypothesis Loop and how does it work?

The Hypothesis Loop is a tool that applies the scientific method to create true market insight from existing data, information and knowledge. It works by testing the brand team's existing understanding of their market and using flaws in that understanding to develop new insights into the market. Those firms that use the Hypothesis Loop effectively do so in five steps.

Step 1: What is it that we don't understand?

Creating new market insight begins with what we don't fully understand but would like to. This step is about creating a simple question, usually about some aspect of customer behaviour. For example:

- Why have customers not switched to our new product?
- Why do customers prefer our competitor?
- Why won't customers pay for added value services around the brand?

The important point at this stage is to translate the business issue—failing to hit targets, for example—into one or more clear questions. A question that has multiple complex answers (e.g. 'Why are we failing to hit target?') will be too broad to provide clear answers.

Step 2: What is our current understanding?

The second step in using the Hypothesis Loop is to make explicit any current beliefs or 'working theories' you currently hold to explain the business situation described in the questions. It's very rare for there to be no such working theories, even if they are only implicit beliefs. Often, there are two or more working theories to explain an issue. It's important that these are made explicit, as in the example in Table 13.1.

Exercise 13.2

Based on your answers in Exercise 13.1, and using Table 13.1 as a guide, make your working theories explicit. Strong answers will be clear and succinct causal explanations that are relevant to the issue in question. Weak answers will be implausible or based on simple prejudice (e.g. the customer prefers the competition because he or she is too bureaucratic to change).

Table 13.1 *Examples of working theories*

QUESTION	WORKING THEORY
Why have customers not switched to our new product?	They aren't aware of its benefits.
Why do customers prefer our competitor?	Their preference is driven by price.
Why won't customers pay for added-value services around the brand?	They don't understand the value created by the services.

The important point at this stage is to understand that if it were correct the working theory would explain the business issue, either fully or in large part. Often, organisations have multiple implicit theories to explain single issues, and making these explicit is a useful exercise.

Exercise 13.3

Building on your answers in Exercises 13.1 and 13.2, develop a pair of hypotheses for each of your working theories. Strong answers will have opposing hypotheses that flow logically from the theory and can be tested by observation. Weak answers will not flow from the working theories, will not have opposing pairs and will not be testable.

Step 3: What hypotheses are suggested by our existing understanding?

Working theories suggest hypotheses about what we should observe in reality. These are predictive statements that can be tested with empirical data. The most useful hypotheses are those expressed in pairs, with the second, null hypothesis being the opposite of the first. The third step in using the Hypothesis Loop is to develop those paired hypotheses from the working theories, as illustrated in Table 13.2.

Table 13.2 *Example pairs of hypotheses developed from working theories*

QUESTION	WORKING THEORY	HYPOTHESIS PAIR
Why have customers not switched to our new product?	They aren't aware of its benefits.	Customers who are aware of our brand's benefits will choose our brand. Customers who are unaware of our brand's benefits will not choose our brand.

QUESTION	WORKING THEORY	HYPOTHESIS PAIR
Why do customers prefer our competitor?	Their preference is driven by price.	The market will be dominated by lower price brands.
		The market will be dominated by higher price brands.
Why won't customers pay for added-value services around the brand?	They don't understand the value created by the services.	Customers who understand the value created by our added-value services will choose to pay for them.
		Customers who don't understand the value created by our added-value services will not choose to pay for them.

The important point at this stage is to ensure that the pairs of hypotheses flow logically from the working theories, are mutually opposed to each other and predict something that can be observed.

Step 4: Are these hypotheses supported by the evidence?

The fourth step in using the Hypothesis Loop is to test the hypotheses using market data that is either already available or can be obtained by some form of market research. This data may be quantitative,

Exercise 13.4

Building on your answers to Exercise 13.3, test your hypotheses using relevant market data. Strong answers will use valid data to clearly confirm or refute each of your working theories. Weak answers will use ambiguous data and neither fully support nor refute your working theories.

qualitative or a combination of both. Importantly, the data needed is dictated by the hypotheses. An example of this is given in Table 13.3.

Table 13.3 *Examples of the testing of working theories and their hypotheses*

QUESTION	WORKING THEORY	HYPOTHESIS PAIR	EMPIRICAL RESULT
Why have customers not switched to our new product?	They aren't aware of its benefits.	Customers who are aware of our brand's benefits will choose our brand. Customers who are unaware of our brand's benefits will not choose our brand.	Comparing brand preference with knowledge of brand benefits supports the hypothesis. Our working theory is supported.
Why do customers prefer our competitor?	Their preference is driven by price.	The market will be dominated by lower price brands. The market will be dominated by higher price brands.	Comparing market shares and pricing supports the null hypothesis. Our working theory is not supported.
Why won't customers pay for added-value services around the brand?	They don't understand the value created by the services.	Customers who understand the value created by our added-value services will choose to pay for them. Customers who don't understand the value created by our added-value services will not choose to pay for them.	Comparing uptake of value-added services with customer understanding of their value supports the null hypothesis. Our working theory is not supported.

The important point at this stage is that the observations made must either confirm or refute your existing working theories. Both outcomes are useful but refutation usually creates better insight than confirmation.

Step 5: What new insight emerges from the loop?

The final step in the Hypothesis Loop is to draw meaning from your testing of the hypotheses. In the case of confirmation this can be straightforward, but refutation of a working theory usually leads to another working theory, which must then be tested by another iteration of the Hypothesis Loop, as shown in Figure 13.3.

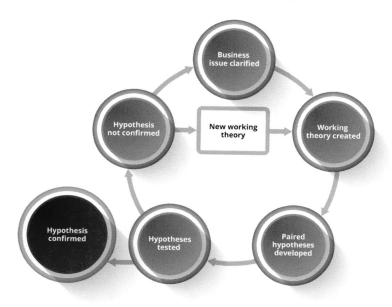

Figure 13.3 *Reiteration of the Hypothesis Loop*

Examples of insights emerging from a Hypothesis Loop are given in Tables 13.4 and 13.5. The important point at this stage is to make sure that the insights drawn are logically consistent with the observations of reality and lead to a better understanding of the market.

Table 13.4 *Examples of insights drawn for confirmation of working theories*

Question	Working theory	Hypothesis pair	Empirical result	Insights drawn
Why have customers not switched to our new product?	They aren't aware of its benefits.	Customers who are aware of our brand's benefits will choose our brand. Customers who are unaware of our brand's benefits will not choose our brand.	Comparing brand preference with knowledge of brand benefits supports the hypothesis. Our working theory is supported.	Our brand benefits are compelling. Our communication of brand benefits is weak.

Table 13.5 *Examples of insights drawn for refutation of working theories*

QUESTION	WORKING THEORY	HYPOTHESIS PAIR	EMPIRICAL RESULT	INSIGHTS DRAWN
Why do customers prefer our competitor?	Their preference is driven by price.	The market will be dominated by lower price brands. The market will be dominated by higher price brands.	Comparing market shares and pricing supports the null hypothesis. Our working theory is not supported.	Price is not a primary market driver. Variation in the share/pricing response suggests that preference is driven by familiarity with usage (new working theory to be tested).
Why won't customers pay for added-value services around the brand?	They don't understand the value created by the services.	Customers who understand the value created by our added-value services will choose to pay for them. Customers who don't understand the value created by our added-value services will not choose to pay for them.	Comparing uptake of value-added services with customer understanding of their value supports the null hypothesis. Our working theory is not supported.	Perceived value of services is not the primary driver of preference for value-added services. Variation in the uptake of services suggests that preference is driven by structuring of customers' budgets (new working theory to be tested).

What should I do with my market insight?

Whether via single iteration or repeated refinement of working theories, the Hypothesis Loop generates new knowledge. If this new knowledge meets the criteria for true market insight (valuable, rare, inimitable and organisationally aligned), then it becomes an important input into the choice of brand strategy. In this way, the Hypothesis Loop complements other tools. It also helps to generate a shared understanding of the market amongst the brand team.

Pragmatic advice for brand leaders

Two practical challenges arise when using the Hypothesis Loop: its method and its inputs. Firstly, the deductive loop process that this tool uses is the same as we use, with great effect, in physical and natural sciences. But it contrasts with the inductive guessing and heuristics we use in everyday life and with which we are instinctively comfortable. This often creates resistance to the deliberate, logical process described here. Of course this is irrational, especially in science-based businesses like pharma and medtech. It is the job of the brand leader to make clear that the scientific method is valuable when applied to brands, just as it is in the lab. The second issue concerns the use of data. Testing hypotheses often involves using multiple and unusual data sources and sometimes gathering new data, which is laborious and creates the objection that the data isn't available. This is a case of the data-provision tail wagging the insight-creation dog. True market insight is incredibly valuable and if the data isn't there to create it then it must be found or gathered. Again, it is the job of the brand leader to make this clear.

Strong brand strategies create value: Using the Concentric Value Proposition to translate strategy into activities

Strong brand strategies create customer preference by following a set of activities that create compelling value for their target customers. This chapter explains how to use the different levels of customer needs to identify a complete set of implementation activities.

When should I use the Concentric Value Proposition?

The Concentric Value Proposition (CVP) translates a brand strategy into activities. Before using it, you must have a strong brand strategy statement using Drucker's Definition (Chapter 3) that has been tested by the Brand Strategy Diagnostics (Chapter 4) and reiterated to be as strong as possible. The brand strategy statement is the main input to the Concentric Value Proposition, but the CVP is also underpinned by the brand team's shared understanding developed throughout the strategy making process. The output is a complete set of activities that are consistent with the brand strategy, coherent with each other and costed within the organisation's resources. Where the CVP fits into the brand strategy process is shown in Figure 14.1.

Figure 14.1 *Where the Concentric Value Proposition fits into the brand strategy process*

Why is the Concentric Value Proposition especially important in pharma and medtech markets?

As with many of the other tools, the CVP is especially important in the pharma and medtech markets because of changes in these markets. Two changes in particular have focused attention on the CVP.

First, historically, pharma and medtech companies have created most of their value through innovative products, but market maturation means it's increasingly difficult to create value by differentiating the core product—the molecule or technology—alone. It's therefore necessary to create value 'beyond the product' in some way. This means identifying additional activity that creates value in the eyes of the customer.

Second, relatively benign competitive conditions in the past allowed so-called 'value-adding' activity to be relatively inefficient, adding cost but making little difference to customer preference. Because of the increased competitive intensity that all pharma and medtech companies now face, it's important that any additional activity creates more value in the eyes of the customer than cost in the eyes of the chief financial officer.

So, the difficulty of differentiating core products and the need to make additional activity truly value-adding makes the CVP especially important in pharma and medtech markets.

What is the Concentric Value Proposition and how does it work?

The CVP is a tool that allows you to identify the activity that would create differential value in the eyes of your target contextual segment. It's based on the idea that value propositions are compelling only when they meet multiple levels of needs. It works by identifying the various levels of value perceived by professionals, payers and patients and translating them into a set of activities that addresses those perceptions. It then tests those activities to determine how they fit with each other and with your brand's implementation resources. Like other brand strategy tools, CVP is as much craft as it is science. Those firms who have mastered it do so in five steps.

Step 1: What are the core needs of our target contextual segment?

Core needs are needs fundamental to the choice of brand. It is essential that the brand strategy addresses these needs, but doing so is

Exercise 14.1

Using Figure 14.2 as a guide, define one of your targeted contextual segments and then define its core needs. Strong answers will identify all significant core needs of patient, payer and prescriber. Weak answers will be incomplete, will fail to address all three customer types and will apply only to some parts of the market rather than the entire market.

sufficient only in embryonic markets, where there is little competition. Core needs typically relate to hygiene factors (see Chapter 5) and the performance of the product. They tend to vary little between contextual segments. An example is shown in Figure 14.2. Note that although this example describes a particular contextual segment, the core needs would be the same for any segment in this market.

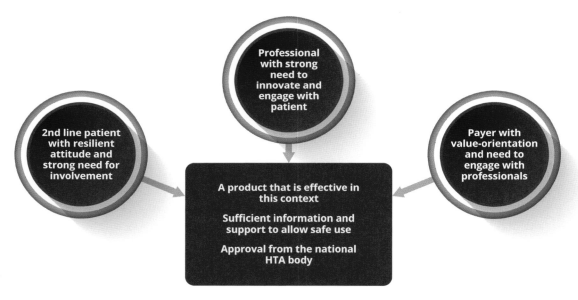

Figure 14.2 *Example of the core needs for a targeted segment*

The important point at this stage is not to omit any hygiene needs that are essential to all of the targeted segment but not to include any motivating needs that are important only to some customers.

Step 2: What are the extended needs of our target contextual segment?

Extended needs are those that are derived directly from the use of the brand. In many markets, the brand's attractiveness is largely determined by the degree to which extended needs are met. Extended needs typically relate to access to and use of the product, and vary between contextual segments. The example in Figure 14.3 uses the same example segment as Figure 14.2.

Exercise 14.2

Using the same contextual segment you used for Exercise 14.1, and Figure 14.3 as a guide, identify your targeted contextual segment's extended needs. Strong answers will identify all significant extended needs of patient, payer and prescriber and be specific to the segment. Weak answers will be incomplete, fail to address all three customer types and apply generally to the market.

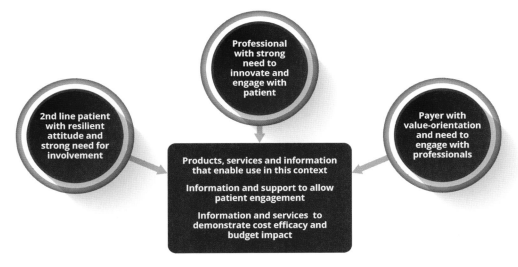

Figure 14.3 *Example of the extended needs for a targeted segment*

At this stage, it's important to not omit any of the targeted segment's extended needs that are directly related to the brand's use and might determine the brand's attractiveness.

Step 3: What are the augmented needs of our target contextual segment?

Augmented needs are those indirectly associated from the use of the brand. In the most competitive markets, when core and extended needs are already fully met by all competitors, the brand's attractiveness is largely determined by the degree to which augmented needs are met. Augmented needs typically relate to customers' intangible, emotional needs around the use of the product and vary greatly between contextual segments. This is shown in the example of Figure 14.4, which again uses the same example contextual segment as used earlier for core and extended needs.

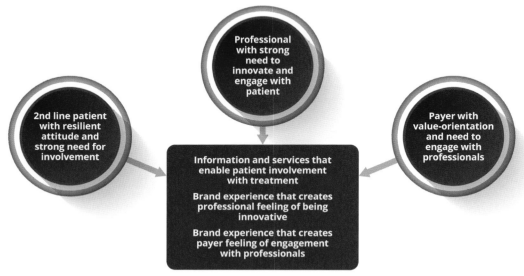

Figure 14.4 *Example of the augmented needs of a targeted segment*

Step 4: What activities will meet the needs of our target contextual segment?

The fourth step in constructing a CVP is to identify the activities required to address the core, extended and augmented needs of the target contextual segment. In theory, the range of possible activities is endless but, in practice, your options are heavily constrained. Constraints include market factors (such as availability of methods to create value and compliance considerations) and internal factors (such as availability of marketing budgets and customer-facing personnel). Working within those constraints, it is essential that each of the core, extended and augmented needs identified in Steps 1, 2 and 3, is addressed by an activity or some combination of activities.

A simplified example of this process of translating needs to activities is given in Figure 14.5. At this stage, it's important to ensure that activities flow from needs, that all needs are addressed and that unnecessary activities, those that don't address core, extended or augmented needs, aren't allowed to divert resources.

Exercise 14.3

Using the same contextual segment as in Exercises 14.1 and 14.2, and using Figure 14.4 as a guide, identify the augmented needs of your targeted contextual segment. Strong answers will identify all significant augmented needs of patient, payer and prescriber and be specific to the segment. Weak answers will be incomplete, will fail to address all three customer types and apply generally to the market rather than to your target segment

Exercise 14.4

Using the results of your work in Steps 1, 2 and 3, and Figure 14.5 as an example, translate your target contextual segment's needs into activities that will address those needs. Strong answers will ensure that the activities address all needs fully. Weak answers will either ignore some needs, meet some needs only partially or suggest activities that aren't related to segment needs.

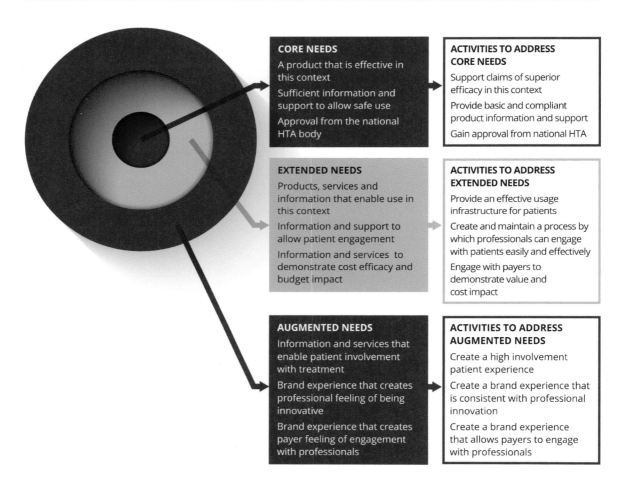

Figure 14.5 *Example of a needs-to-activity translation*

Step 5: How strong is our value proposition?

The CVP is the aggregation of all the value-creating activities identified in Step 4. These activities are necessary to meet the needs of your target contextual segment. A strong CVP substantiates the offer to that segment, as defined in your brand strategy statement. The final step in the CVP process is to assess the probability that your target contextual segment will prefer it to any competing value propositions. To determine your CVP's strength, use the 4C Test, shown in Figure 14.6.

Exercise 14.5

Using Figure 14.6 as a guide, assess the strength of the list of activities you developed in Exercise 14.4. A strong answer will provide evidence that all four tests are met or recommendations for how the list of activities can be improved. A weak answer will provide little evidence or will apply only some of the tests.

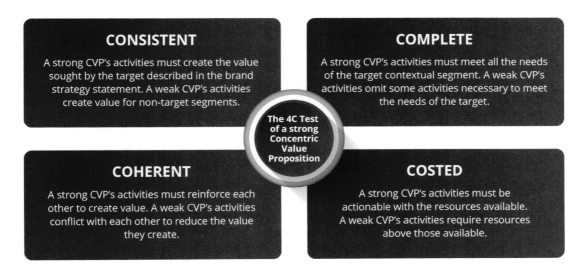

CONSISTENT

A strong CVP's activities must create the value sought by the target described in the brand strategy statement. A weak CVP's activities create value for non-target segments.

COMPLETE

A strong CVP's activities must meet all the needs of the target contextual segment. A weak CVP's activities omit some activities necessary to meet the needs of the target.

The 4C Test of a strong Concentric Value Proposition

COHERENT

A strong CVP's activities must reinforce each other to create value. A weak CVP's activities conflict with each other to reduce the value they create.

COSTED

A strong CVP's activities must be actionable with the resources available. A weak CVP's activities require resources above those available.

Figure 14.6 *The 4C Test of a strong Concentric Value Proposition*

The assessment of a CVP's strength is necessarily a judgement rather than a measurement but it's greatly enhanced by using the 4C Test, which addresses the most common weaknesses found in practice.

What should I do with my Concentric Value Proposition?

The output of the Concentric Value Proposition is a list of activities that will create value for and the preference of the target contextual segment. This list provides the inputs for two other tools: 3L Metrics (Chapter 15) and the Wedge Brand Plan Structure (Chapter 16). In addition, applying the CVP tool develops in the brand team a shared view of what's needed and a commitment to implementation.

Pragmatic advice for brand leaders

The idea behind CVP is not controversial: our activities must be valuable to the target segment and so win their preference. Despite this, two practical problems come up in execution. The first is that, in the leap from brand strategy statement to activity planning, brand teams often forget the Drucker Definition of strategy and revert to addressing the market (e.g. disease area, product category) rather than the target contextual segment. Since a market consists of many segments with varying needs, the resultant mix of activities is always a fudge that tries to please all customers and, in doing so, delights nobody. The job of the brand leader is to keep the brand team focused on the needs of the target contextual segment, not the market overall. The second problem is pet project syndrome. This occurs when the carefully developed, 4C-tested CVP doesn't include some activity to which the brand team is emotionally committed, such as a currently fashionable fad. This often results in the twisting of the CVP's logic to accommodate the pet project, even if value isn't created. It is the job of the brand leader to avoid pet project syndrome and ensure the CVP is designed rationally.

Strong brand strategies are measured: Using 3L Metrics to improve brand strategy implementation

Strong brand strategies are implemented dynamically, adapting to new information and becoming stronger with each planning cycle. This chapter explains how different kinds of metrics allow effective implementation of your brand strategy.

When should I use 3L Metrics?

Metrics are essential to the implementation any brand strategy and 3L Metrics are essential to any but the simplest brand strategy. Their design begins with the list of activities developed through the Concentric Value Proposition (Chapter 14). The output of using the 3L Metrics tool is a dashboard of tangible measures that enables you not only to measure the success of your strategy but also to take corrective action during implementation and to improve the next iteration of your brand strategy. Figure 15.1 shows where the 3L Metrics tool fits into the brand strategy process.

Figure 15.1 *Where 3L Metrics fit into the brand strategy process*

Why are 3L Metrics especially important in pharma and medtech markets?

Whilst measuring the results of strategy is not a new idea, the evolution of pharma and medtech markets has changed what sort of metrics we need in two important ways.

First, this evolution has increased pressure for results. Increased costs of bringing a new device or drug to market, greater competitive intensity and new commercial risks, such as market access, have combined to make investors more interested in performance. Compared to those of an earlier generation, these investors need more reassurance that your brand strategy has delivered on its promises and will continue to do so.

Second, this evolution has accelerated market change. As both the technological and social environments evolve (see Chapter 11), brand strategies become more vulnerable to being overtaken by change. As a result, brand teams need the information that will enable them to adapt their strategies not only at regular strategy reviews but also during implementation.

So, more demanding investors on the one side and rapidly changing markets on the other make 3L Metrics especially important in pharma and medtech markets.

What are 3L Metrics and how do they work?

The 3L Metrics tool is a framework for deciding what to measure as you implement your brand strategy. It's based on the idea that you are concerned with performance in the past, present and future. This leads to three types of metrics, as shown in Figure 15.2.

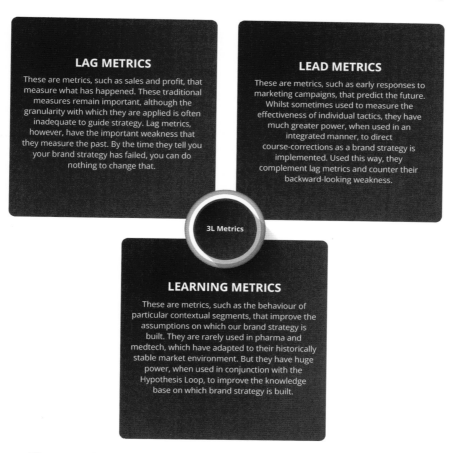

LAG METRICS

These are metrics, such as sales and profit, that measure what has happened. These traditional measures remain important, although the granularity with which they are applied is often inadequate to guide strategy. Lag metrics, however, have the important weakness that they measure the past. By the time they tell you your brand strategy has failed, you can do nothing to change that.

LEAD METRICS

These are metrics, such as early responses to marketing campaigns, that predict the future. Whilst sometimes used to measure the effectiveness of individual tactics, they have much greater power, when used in an integrated manner, to direct course-corrections as a brand strategy is implemented. Used this way, they complement lag metrics and counter their backward-looking weakness.

3L Metrics

LEARNING METRICS

These are metrics, such as the behaviour of particular contextual segments, that improve the assumptions on which our brand strategy is built. They are rarely used in pharma and medtech, which have adapted to their historically stable market environment. But they have huge power, when used in conjunction with the Hypothesis Loop, to improve the knowledge base on which brand strategy is built.

Figure 15.2 *The three perspectives of performance measurement*

179

Exercise 15.1

Using your brand strategy statement from Chapter 2, and guided by Figure 15.3, define the lag metrics that would tell you if your brand strategy has been a success or not. Strong answers will define sales, profit and other measures for each contextual segment but especially the Focus and Maintain segments. Weak answers will define measures by product, geography or account that give no indication of brand strategy success at contextual segment level.

The 3L Metrics framework is more sophisticated than that used by most pharma and medtech companies, which rely heavily on lag metrics. Firms that use this approach successfully do so in four steps:

Step 1: What lag metrics do we need to measure successful implementation?

Typical practice in most pharma and medtech companies is to measure lag indicators—such as profit and sales in volume and value—by product, geography, account, etc. These metrics are used because they are easy to measure and are needed in any case for financial and operational reasons. But, no matter how detailed, this data contains almost no information about your brand strategy's implementation or success as defined in the brand strategy statement (Chapter 2).

Effective measurement of strategy success requires that you measure what the strategy aims to do. This means measuring the same lag indicators, but structured by contextual segment. In practice, this requires the integration of product sales data with customer profiling data, a process that is now possible with the use of sales force automation software. An example of this is given in Figure 15.3.

Figure 15.3 *Example of data integration to measure lag indicators by contextual segment*

Step 2: What lead metrics do we need to guide course-corrections?

The activities that are the output of the Concentric Value Proposition (CVP) are necessary to create value for and the preference of the target contextual segment. Each of these activities has a desired final outcome and also a number of implementation milestones that precede the final outcome. For example, an activity such as a series of professional meetings to support a product launch is expected to generate a number of expressions of interest, a number of trial users and then a number of committed users. Using a small number of reasonable assumptions, it's possible to work backwards from lag indicators to the desired final outcome and preliminary outcomes of each activity, as in the simplified example in Figure 15.4.

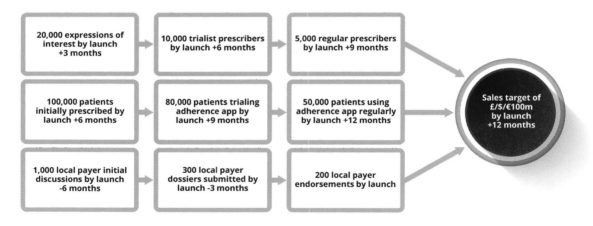

Fig 15.4 *Example of lead indicators developed from a lag indicator*

By performing a similar retrogression on all the major activities developed through the CVP, you can identify what factors to measure as good predictors of future outcomes.

Variance of any lead indicators from the target informs course-corrections, such as the need to increase, decrease or modify resource allocation. For example, a shortfall in the conversion of interested customers to trialists might indicate spending more time on following up those interested customers.

Step 3: What learning metrics do we need to improve our market understanding?

Even the best brand strategies involve some assumptions, either implicit or explicit. Assumptions may be necessary in any part of your planning, including, for example, the relative sizes of contextual segments, how they will behave or the impact of competitor activity. Each of these assumptions are potential weaknesses in your brand strategy, and improving them with evidence would make the next iteration of your brand strategy stronger and more likely to succeed. Examples of such assumptions, developed from a typical strategy, are given in Table 15.1.

Exercise 15.2

Using the list of activities generated by using the Concentric Value Proposition, select the activities that you think are most critical to the success of your brand strategy. Then, using Figure 15.4 as a guide, and the outcomes of Exercise 15.1, work backwards from your lag indicators to construct a series of lead indicators. Strong answers will identify lead indicators that are consistent with the lag indicator for each major activity and will also inform any corrective action. Weak answers will define lead indicators that are not consistent with the lag indicator and don't inform corrective action.

Table 15.1 *Examples of planning assumptions and associated learning metrics*

COMPONENT OF BRAND STRATEGY STATEMENT	INHERENT ASSUMPTION	HYPOTHESIS PAIR	LEARNING METRICS
Build the value proposition to Contextual Segment A by developing a method to aggregate and share real-world data (RWD) to support cost-effective indications.	The ability to use RWD to better target use of this product would shift customer preference in this contextual segment.	Payers who are introduced to the extended, RWD based value proposition during development will significantly prefer the product to competitors'. Payers who have not been introduced to the extended, RWD based value proposition during development will show no change in their preference.	Variations in preference between payers exposed to the value proposition and those not
Focus on Contextual Segment B with a value proposition based around compliance and compliance-related outcomes.	Preference in Contextual Segment B is primarily driven by compliance and compliance-related outcomes.	Customers in Contextual Segment B who experience great compliance and better compliance-related outcomes will show higher preference for our product. Customers in Contextual Segment B who experience poor compliance and poorer compliance-related outcomes will show lower preference for our product.	Variations in preference between customers in Contextual Segment B with differing levels of compliance and compliance-related outcomes

COMPONENT OF BRAND STRATEGY STATEMENT	INHERENT ASSUMPTION	HYPOTHESIS PAIR	LEARNING METRICS
Maintain Contextual Segment C by selectively withdrawing resources and service.	Preference in Contextual Segment C isn't influenced by those resources or that service.	Customers in Contextual Segment C will remain loyal after withdrawal of resources. Customers in Contextual Segment C will switch to competitors after withdrawal of resources.	Variations in usage by Contextual Segment C following removal of resources and service
Opportune Contextual Segment D by withdrawing all sales and marketing activity.	Preference in Contextual Segment D isn't influenced by sales and marketing activity.	Usage by Contextual Segment D won't vary after withdrawal of sales and marketing activity. Usage by Contextual Segment D will vary after withdrawal of sales and marketing activity.	Variations in usage by Contextual Segment D following withdrawal of sales and marketing activity

Learning metrics are factors that are measured so that you can apply the Hypothesis Loop (see Chapter 13). They are chosen according to what is needed to test the hypothesis pair used in that tool, as shown in the simplified example of Table 15.1. Learning metrics like these are only used by the most sophisticated

Exercise 15.3

Using Table 15.1 as a guide, identify the most important assumptions that are inherent in your brand strategy; then, referring to the Hypothesis Loop (Chapter 13), develop relevant paired hypotheses and learning metrics to test them. Strong answers will identify measurable learning indicators for each important assumption. Weak answers will do this only for some assumptions.

pharma and medtech companies but they are a powerful way to improve your brand strategy's adaptation to a changing market environment.

Step 4: What do we need to measure?

The final step in developing 3L Metrics is to collate the necessary lag, lead and learning metrics into a comprehensive dashboard. This involves gathering them together and assigning expected values to them. In addition, the lead indicators should include plans for corrective action if they're outside expected parameters. Obviously, this involves gathering the outcomes of Steps 1, 2 and 3, and the content of the dashboard is very case specific. It should look different for every strategy.

What should I do with my 3L Metrics?

The outcome of using the 3L Metrics tool is a comprehensive set of lag, learning and lead indicators. In practice, these complement rather than replace the traditional product-based lag indicators used by most companies and that remain important for operational reasons. These metrics feed into the Wedge Brand Plan Structure (Chapter 16) but, importantly, they should be actively used to enable the implementation of brand strategy, to make course-corrections and to improve the next iteration of the brand strategy.

Pragmatic advice for brand leaders

In practice, application of the 3L Metrics tool runs into two related issues that the brand leader must address. The first is that the traditional metrics of product sales and profit by geography, account etc. will remain in place. They are deeply embedded in the organisational culture and remain necessary for operational reasons, even though they are unhelpful in strategy implementation. Therefore, 3L Metrics must run alongside the traditional system and will appear to bring more work and complexity. The brand leader must overcome resistance to this by making clear that 3L Metrics are essential to brand strategy implementation. The second issue is that of information availability. Whilst the traditionally structured data is readily available, some of the information required for 3L Metrics will not be. This creates the preference for using easily available but less useful data over using less accessible but essential data. Resistance to change will come from both data providers (business information, finance) and data users (the brand team and sales team). Again, it is the job of the brand leader to overcome this resistance by stressing the necessity to implement the brand strategy well in a changing market.

Strong brand strategies are understood: Using the Wedge Brand Plan Structure to communicate your brand strategy

Strong brand strategies are fully understood by those who must support and implement them. This chapter explains how to structure your brand plan so that it will be read, committed to and implemented.

When should I use the Wedge Brand Plan Structure?

The brand plan can only be written once the market is defined and analysed, the brand strategy defined and developed into activities and 3L Metrics set. The Wedge Brand Plan Structure tool is applicable in any situation where the brand strategy isn't trivially simple. In pharma and medtech, this means that almost all brand plans would benefit from this structure. It takes the outputs of all the other tools described in this book and turns them in a document that can be read and used to support implementation. The place of the Wedge Brand Plan Structure in the brand planning process is shown in Figure 16.1.

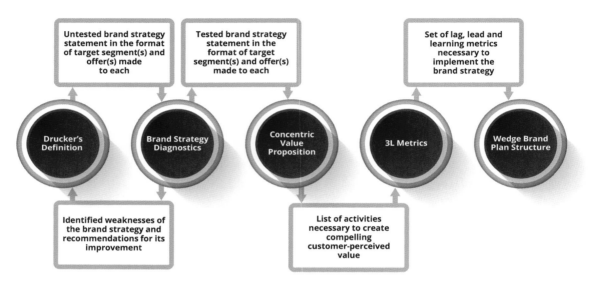

Figure 16.1 *Where the Wedge Brand Plan Structure fits into the brand strategy process*

Why is the Wedge Brand Plan Structure especially important in pharma and medtech markets?

The Wedge Brand Plan Structure is relevant to any brand strategy but it is especially relevant in pharma and medtech because of the dysfunctional structure of brand plans currently used by many companies. The traditionally structured brand plan typically has three major faults.

Firstly, it's a huge, dense document. This means that it is ineffective as a communication medium. An effective brand plan structure is readable, whilst still containing all the necessary information.

Secondly, it puts all the detail first. This means that the important points are lost in the detail and the reader must work hard to find what is important. An effective brand plan makes it easy to find the key points and any necessary supporting information.

Finally, it rarely states the brand strategy explicitly according to Drucker's Definition. As a result, the reader must infer the strategy from a mass of tactical detail. An effective brand plan makes the strategy stand out from the tactical detail.

Given that the primary function of the brand plan is to communicate the brand strategy, these three common failings mean many pharma and medtech brand plans are not fit for purpose. This wastes significant resources both directly (the cost of creating plans that don't fulfil their purpose) and indirectly (the cost of weak implementation of poorly understood plans). Lack of fitness for purpose and consequent wasted resources is why the Wedge Brand Plan Structure is especially important in pharma and medtech.

What is the Wedge Brand Plan Structure and how does it work?

The Wedge Brand Plan Structure tool is a format for writing brand plans that presents information in a wedge-like manner. There is first a 'sharp end'—a small amount of information that is essential to read. This is followed by a much larger amount of supporting information that can be read only if necessary and to different degrees by different audiences. The structure works by concentrating essential information into a readable volume—typically four to six pages—and connecting it to supporting information in the detailed set of appendices. This separation of essential from supporting information is a skilled task. Brand teams that have mastered it structure their plans as shown in Figure 16.2 and described below.

Figure 16.2 *Outline of the Wedge Brand Plan Structure*

Executive summary

The executive summary is a paragraph of less than 200 words that is limited to:

- a statement of which brand(s) the plan covers and any geographical or sectoral constraints
- a distillation of the brand strategy statement

- a statement of those new activities that will contribute significantly to achieving customer preference, and
- a quantified statement of both resources expended and returns expected

The executive summary doesn't need to cross-reference any other part of the brand plan.

Critical success factors

This section restates the 6 to 10 critical success factors from the SWOT Alignment. These typically occupy about half a page but they are closely referenced to the various supporting appendices which provide the inputs into the SWOT Alignment.

Brand strategy statement

This should appear in Drucker's Definition format. It typically occupies no more than a few lines but cross-references the appendices, which include the Brand Strategy Diagnostics, the SWOT Alignment and the Focus Matrix.

Activity plan

This is a brief description of activities most important to the brand strategy or that require large shifts in resource allocation. This section is typically one or two pages but cross-references the appendices, especially the Concentric Value Proposition, which must justify the activities using the 4C Test.

Metrics

This section should contain headline statements of the following metrics:

- traditional lag metrics (e.g. spend and return structured by product and geography)
- lag metrics by contextual segment
- lead metrics for key activities and derived from lag metrics and
- learning metrics for key planning assumptions.

This section is typically one or two pages but cross-references appendices such as market data, targets and 3L Metrics.

Appendices

The number and type of appendices in this section will be case dependent. In almost all cases, this section should include appendices with full details of the work carried out with the following tools:

Exercise 16.1

Critique your current brand plan against four criteria.

1. **How well it separates the critical success factors your brand strategy must address from the mass of detail about the market.**
2. **How clearly it states your brand strategy, in Drucker's Definition format, as distinct from the background to the strategy and the activity associated with it.**
3. **How easy it is for those responsible for approving the plan to understand the strategy and constructively challenge it.**
4. **How well it allows those responsible for implementing the plan to understand it and play their part in implementation.**

Strong answers will identify where the Wedge Brand Plan Structure might improve the brand plan in regard to all four criteria. Weak answers will not find ways to improve the existing brand plan structure.

- Emergent Properties Analysis
- Competitive Pressure Analysis
- Contextual Segmentation
- Value Chain Comparison
- Product Category Life Cycle
- Hypothesis Loop
- Reality Filters
- SWOT Alignment
- Focus Matrix
- Concentric Value Proposition, including the 4C Test
- 3L Metrics
- Brand Strategy Diagnostic

Exercise 16.2

Using the results of all the other exercises in this book, prepare a draft version of your brand plan using the Wedge Brand Plan Structure. Strong answers will engage the brand team in doing this. Weak answers will allow habits and cultural constraints to prevent significant change in practice.

This section should also include the brand strategy statement, as well as market data and financial data.

A very important point in constructing the plan is that the essential information section is heavily cross linked to the exact places in each of the appendices where supporting evidence is provided. In this way, the balance between a document brief enough to communicate and one extensive enough to refer to is achieved.

Pragmatic advice for brand leaders

Many brand teams and their colleagues describe the brand planning process as unsatisfactory, the planning cycle as a political game and the final document as being of limited use. Despite this, the habits of writing poorly structured brand plans are deeply ingrained in pharma and medtech companies, whose plan format and content is usually remarkably similar. The brand leader faces two challenges in changing this situation. The first is the comfort of the old way of doing things, even if those ways are ineffective. Attempting to change how brand planning is done often results in the old habits being maintained with only cosmetic changes. The second is the fear of the new way of doing things. Learning new tools, like the ones described in this book, is an intellectual and emotional challenge that brand team members usually say they relish but, in fact, they often fear. These two challenges, comfort in the old and fear of the new, are what prevents your brand team and your company from changing. The brand leader, along with senior colleagues, can make change happen. Without leadership from the brand leader, change is impossible.

Appendix: Further reading

Like all substantive books, *Brand Therapy* is built on deep underpinnings of earlier work, both that of seminal thinkers in the strategy field generally and my own original research, which focuses specifically on strategy in pharma, medtech and other life science markets. In my previous books these foundations are made clear in extensive bibliographies; but because *Brand Therapy* isn't an academic book this didn't seem appropriate here. This book's intended readers are unlikely to search for and read the massive amount of material that I, as an academic researcher, spend my life reading. Instead, this Appendix points out only the most relevant and useful publications that might interest the reader. The books can be found on Amazon or other bookshops. The shorter articles for which I have copyright are highlighted in red; these (and hundreds of others) are available at www.pragmedic.com.

Chapter 2: Using the Customer-Centric Market Definition to frame your analysis

Customer-centricity, sometimes called patient-centricity, is an idea that emerged from the great flowering of marketing thought in the 1950s. Whilst much of what has been written on the subject in recent years is self-serving hype from consultancies, the thinking of the early writers remains worth reading for its clarity, focus and rigour. Of these, Theodore Levitt is my personal favourite and the best, most readable collection of his work is *The Marketing Imagination*, published by Free Press in 1986.

Chapter 3: Using Drucker's Definition to clarify your brand strategy

I developed the definition of brand strategy from the work of dozens of great thinkers: theorists such as Henry Mintzberg, Shelby D. Hunt and Richard Rumelt, and those who defined the strategic marketing planning process, such as Philip Kotler and Malcolm McDonald. But Peter Drucker's work was the most influential and, although you won't find my definition verbatim in his work, he deserves the appellation. If you would like to know more about what brand strategy is, you can find an extensive treatment in my first book *Making Marketing Happen*, published by Elsevier in 2005.

Chapter 4: Using Brand Strategy Diagnostics to test and improve your strategy

The differences between strategies that work and those that don't had been noted by various researchers for decades, but I developed them into a diagnostic tool while I was working on my PhD, in the early 2000s. You can find much more detail on these differences in *Making Marketing Happen* and in *Marketing and Finance*, written with Malcolm McDonald and Keith Ward, published by Wiley in 2013. I also wrote a series of shorter, more industry-specific papers—The Effectiveness of Marketing Strategy Making Processes (2002), An Empirical Investigation of Marketing Strategy Quality in Medical Markets (2003), Success and Failure in Marketing Strategy Making (2003) and Excellence in Medical Marketing (2007)—which appeared in the Journal of Targeting, Measurement and Analysis for Marketing; I've also published many short articles on the idea of testing strategies before implementation, including Testing Times, which appeared in *Clinica* (2012).

Chapter 5: Using SWOT Alignment to guide your brand strategy

I developed SWOT Alignment, and you can read more about it in *Making Marketing Happen* and *Marketing and Finance*. A shorter summary article was published as Competing on Alignment in *PharmaFocus Asia* (2015).

Chapter 6: Using Reality Filters to gain strategic objectivity

The idea of testing the inputs into the SWOT Alignment is my own work but it builds on a body of knowledge called the Resourced Based View. In particular, the ideas behind the filters owe a lot to the work of Jay Barney, especially his excellent book *Gaining and Sustaining Competitive Advantage*, published by Prentice Hall in 2001.

Chapter 7: Using the Focus Matrix to guide complex strategies

The idea of focusing effort on the basis of attractiveness and winnability is an old one. It precedes the Ansoff Matrix (1957) and the Boston Consulting Group Matrix (1965). Most strategic management textbooks talk about the operationalisation of this approach and I've been especially influenced by Malcolm McDonald, who was my PhD supervisor, and his excellent text *Marketing Plans* (Elsevier, 2016). To the best of my knowledge, however, *Brand Therapy* is the first to apply it specifically to pharma and medtech markets.

Chapter 8: Using Value Chain Comparison to identify your firm's distinctive strengths and weaknesses

The value chain concept is the brainchild of Michael Porter and was first described in his hugely influential book *Competitive Advantage*, published by Free Press in 1985. Porter's idea has been used to describe the pharma and medtech industry in various consultancy reports but, to the best of my knowledge, *Brand Therapy* is the first to use it to elucidate putative strengths and weaknesses.

Chapter 9: Using Competitive Pressure Analysis to identify competitive threats and opportunities

Competitive Pressure Analysis is an industry-specific tool that I developed from Michael Porter's Five Forces model, published in *Harvard Business Review* (1979). And in 2017, *Chartered Marketer* published my succinct article on the idea: Force Protection.

Chapter 10: Using Contextual Segmentation to identify opportunities and threats from customer differences

Segmentation has been written about for decades and I have been particularly influenced by the work of Philip Kotler and Malcolm McDonald. The concept of Contextual Segmentation involving payers, professionals and patients is an original idea of my own. A short summary of it is given in Superior Segmentation, published in *Pharmaceutical Marketing Europe* (*PME*) (2012). A description of the failings of most segmentation in the life sciences is reported in Mindset and Marketing Segmentation in the *Journal of Medical Marketing* (2006).

Chapter 11: Using Emergent Properties Analysis to identify future opportunities and threats

Emergent Properties Analysis is derived from my work applying evolutionary theory to the life sciences industry. It's described at length in my books *The Future of Pharma* and *Darwin's Medicine*, published by Taylor and Francis (2011 and 2016 respectively). Short summaries of the forces shaping the industry are given in Under Pressure in *PME* (2016) and Megatrends in *Clinica* (2012).

Chapter 12: Using the Product Category Life Cycle to predict customer and competitor behaviour

In our industry, life cycle analyses at the product category level are rare. A review of the literature and the implication for medtech markets can be found in Product Life Cycle in Medical Technology Innovation, in *Journal of Medical Marketing* (2013). Shorter summaries can be found in Life Cycle Management, in *Clinica* (2012) and Life Story, in *PharmaFocus Asia* (2017).

Chapter 13: Using the Hypothesis Loop to see what your competitors don't

The Hypothesis Loop has its origins in the work of Agyris and Schon, but the ideas in this chapter come from a large research study that I reported in my book with Paul Raspin, *Creating Market Insight*, published by Wiley (2006). Articles on this topic include The 12 Rules of Customer Insight, in the *Journal of Medical Marketing* (2006) and Transform into Value, in *PME* (2008).

Chapter 14: Using the Concentric Value Proposition to translate strategy into activities

Although the idea of value propositions is discussed in most strategic management textbooks, its application to pharma and medtech in this way—based on the contextual segment's needs and developed in layers—is unique to *Brand Therapy*. I've also published short articles on the subject: Modern Values, in *PME* (2013) and Lessons on the Value of Service, in *Clinica* (2014).

Chapter 15: Using 3L Metrics to improve brand strategy implementation

Extensive literature on both metrics and organisational learning exists, but these things are rarely connected to each other. The concept of 3L Metrics is my synthesis of traditional metrics with those needed for organisational learning, as discussed in *Creating Market Insight* (2006). This chapter is the first publication of my work on 3L Metrics, although a short article, The Lasting Advantage, appeared in *PharmaFocus Asia* (2015).

Chapter 16: Using the Wedge Brand Plan Structure to communicate your brand strategy

My work on the structuring of brand plans began with the work of Philip Kotler and Malcolm McDonald, who have both written extensively on the subject. This chapter is the first publication of my ideas on the Wedge Brand Plan Structure, which I developed through working with a number of pharma and medtech companies.

Printed in Great Britain
by Amazon